A BRIDGE NOT TOO FAR

A BRIDGE NOT TOO FAR

DEEPAK OHRI

CEO of lebua Hotels and Resorts

Waterside Productions

Bangkok   2023

First Printing: 2023

ISBN-13: 978-1-957807-83-6 hardcover edition
ISBN-13: 978-1-957807-84-3 e-book edition

Interior book design by Claudine Mansour Design

Printed in the United States of America

Waterside Productions
2055 Oxford Ave
Cardiff, CA 92007

www.waterside.com

To my late father, M. L. Ohri, and my mother, Vijay Ohri.
I am who I am because of their love and encouragement.

TABLE OF CONTENTS

PREFACE

It is said that we are the sum total of our life experiences. My journey has been a roller coaster of ups and downs, from humble beginnings to present day. All my successes are built on a foundation of failures. I have followed a path that has brought me a sense of achievement based on sound judgement and innovative ideas. There have been struggles, mistakes, as well as supportive teachers who have guided me through the tough times. Mine is a simple story of a young boy with big dreams, and the journey of self-discovery through challenges and facing my fears. It is often during the toughest times of our lives that we gain insights into how to swim in deep waters and survive the turbulent parts of life.

The hyper-competitiveness of any line of work requires you to make snap decisions and to execute them with conviction. Some of the decisions I made were risky; they teetered on a make-or-break moment. Many decisions were so out-of-the-box, that even today, when I speak to students at business schools, they cannot conceptualize the success of those decisions. Yet my methods have proven successful through the years.

I hold in esteem all of the people who have crossed my path and given me the strength to stand up for my values. My personality has been both a flaw and a favor. We are all colored by our values or beliefs and influenced by our environment. We make choices and decisions based on what we think is right. As we evolve, we alter our thought processes, and change with time.

Time. The one important factor that I believe is more powerful than even God. I believe that even the Divine would agree that time is the ultimate challenger of our lives. We must bow to time, to its ability to give and take opportunities. I would say that time has been on my side; or rather I have been open to myriad opportunities, as if the unseen hands of fate nudged me in a certain direction right when I needed it. Many such prospects have come to me at the right time, in the right way, and I believe for the right reasons—either to learn or to teach.

Time. The one important factor that I believe is more powerful than even God.

When I asked myself what the true essence of an entrepreneur is—business goals and ambition, work and leadership—I realized something important. The driving force for each one of us is unique. What fuels your passion is not the same as what fuels mine. Listening deeply to our inner selves and to our mentors and loved ones makes us realize that we are not merely existing but also creating and building one simple dream upon another.

We all thrive on ambition: it feeds us and offers us shelter and gives us a sense of self-worth to lead fulfilling lives. We face challenges that teach us to grow, to unmask the illusions, and be recognized for our true nature. We extract meaning from every incident in our journey toward achievement. We discover more about ourselves so we can become who we want to be.

THE LUXURY PHENOMENON

"One of the biggest trends in the modern luxury market is the shifting focus toward experiences over material things. By 2022, the Boston Consulting Group predicts that personal and experiential luxury alone will be a €1,135 billion market—a 34 percent increase from 2015. This may be partly due to the view that experiences are harder to commodify—meaning they are more likely to be authentic. Travel to remote parts of the world, and memorable interactions with genuine people represent a kind of rarity that is irreproducible."[1]

Luxury is an experience that creates memories for a lifetime. Every simple joy can be a luxury. Happiness exists in moments. Cherished memories and unique experiences bring joy, and that is the true luxury. I've always aspired to improve upon a very simple idea: to make people exceptionally happy through food, drink, and service. I have taken this concept to a different level. It is my deep conviction that the power of service and hospitality is what enriches people's lives and brings them a certain joy. This is what I believe should be the ultimate goal of anyone who is in this industry, but it should also be the end goal for anyone in any industry. Hospitality is not about running a hotel impersonally, but dealing with every aspect with *sincerity*, to ensure that the hotel or restaurant provides the best service every second of every day.

I believe that hospitality is what I was born to do—it is my destiny. Despite it being one of the toughest businesses, it became easy for me once I understood that hospitality is centered

---

1 "What Does Luxury Mean Today?," Local Measure, April 18, 2017, https://www.localmeasure.com/post/luxury-mean-today.

around two fundamentals: employees and customers. It is all about building relationships founded on respect and understanding. Recognizing these two key values, trust became the natural direction which then developed into long-term loyalty.

To be a successful restaurateur and CEO of a luxury hotel, you need to know what it feels like to be a dishwasher, waiter, cook, employee, and executive. You also need to intrinsically understand the needs of the customer, and then meet and exceed those expectations. I enjoy the challenge this represents. Setting my sights really high ignites a burning desire to design a service that would add value to a person's life. I have worked hard to carve out a niche for myself, and for others who have come after me. I achieved my goals on my own terms and that is really the key to my success. Self-respect serves as my anchor; it is the "why" that has kept me grounded. I choose to lead my life with conviction.

I admit I am a bit of a maverick, and many people have called me arrogant and proud. It might even be true. People see my success as the result of *lebua*. But I am more than that. With this book, I hope to reveal the deeper side of Deepak Ohri, the man who is independent of any brand.

FINAL THOUGHTS

As events unfolded in my work life, not everyone has seen eye-to-eye with me. And that is perfectly fine. The important point is that I had conviction in the face of others' doubts. I stood strong to deliver on what I envisioned, which eventually led to a successful reality. I share my journey now because I want others to see the world as I see it and embrace the philosophy that has enabled me to find such immense success.

Your own journey will undoubtably be one of ups and downs,

failures and successes. It will require you to cope with disappointments and face reality with the courage to rise up and be successful in spite of it. Practical, not theoretical, skills are necessary to understand how we function when facing adverse moments. When you are successful, people don't notice your failures and struggles; they don't notice the way you powered through terrible loss, or how you suffered through insults and enmity. What's important is that you keep going. Every step of your journey is headed to a bridge not too far.

INTRODUCTION

*"A good father is a source of
    inspiration and self-restraint.
    A good mother is the root of
    kindness and humbleness."*

—DR T.P. CHIA

I am different.

At least, that's what many people say. Whenever I speak at conferences, or work with aspiring graduate students, or advise entrepreneurs, people comment on my ability to view problems from a unique perspective. There are many other leaders, entrepreneurs, and insightful executives who have shared their vision and their understanding of this world, but what makes my story unique is how I came to have this different viewpoint from which I look at businesses and the world.

That's what is the most unique in anyone's journey—their roots. Why I am the way I am today was shaped by my childhood. It really comes down to the influence my father had on my life. He was my inspiration and my teacher. My father was a man who painted the blank canvas of my mind and taught me to think and behave differently. He was a man I respected more than any other. When my father became ill and knew his time had come to leave this earth, he gave me some precious advice.

For a long time, my father had brushed aside any suggestion that anything was wrong with his health. However, my wife and I learned from my mother and his doctor that he needed immediate medical attention; his kidneys were failing. I gently suggested to my father that it would be better if he came to Bangkok for a visit. He was reluctant. He was a proud and independent man, and he didn't want to be dependent on us. However, he finally relented under the condition that they would not stay for more than a week.

When he was examined in Bangkok, we learned he would have to stay longer. He had to go for procedures twice a week, and I went with him. Those few years with my father, twice a week, two hours together, transformed me. My father's wisdom gave me pause for thought. If we have the capacity to change ourselves, we can make a difference in our society. More importantly, if we put humanity ahead of material gains, place the value of people above profit and loss, then we can discover compassion and learn to reciprocate love and care.

My father passed away on October 31st, 2019. Twelve hours before he passed, he shared that one important lesson: "Never forget your roots."

MY ROOTS

My father wasn't a rich man, but to me, he was richer than anybody else in the world. He was the man behind my ideals and values, and who, to this day, I owe everything. He worked overtime to ensure we had enough to overcome the rising costs of living. My mother was adept at keeping expenses to a minimum. She would darn our clothes, shine our shoes, and ensure we looked neat and tidy before we went to school. No one needed to know that at times my parents struggled with a meager monthly income.

We didn't consider our family to be poor, but we were not exactly able to afford a flat with separate rooms either. We had one single square space cordoned off by curtains. My mother planned the layout of the kitchen, living room, and bathing area. We had no air-conditioning, just a squeaky fan and the hand-held straw fans my mother used while we would eat. In the corner, there was a clay pot dispenser that kept our drinking water cool.

One day, when I was six or seven years old, my father took me to the shops. Going out to the market to experience the crowded hustle of city life, filled with cyclists, pedestrians, and roadside vendors, felt like an adventure. I loved all the shiny cars. Back in the 1970s, there were only two brands of cars: Fiat and Ambassador. They rumbled through the roads with horns honking. Only the rich could afford such a luxury. I wanted to have a car like that someday, so I, too, could proudly drive through the streets.

That day, which is still etched in my memory, my father and I headed to the shirt shop in the market to purchase a shirt. His were old and worn out, and he wanted to get a new one for himself. Next to the shirt shop was a toy store. Like all kids, I was enraptured by the toys in the display window. I caught sight of a miniature milk van and I just *had* to have it. I fell in love with that little white vehicle. I tugged my father's hand toward the toy shop. I pointed to that little white van. My father, tall, stoic, and intimidating, knelt down on one knee and looked at me. He saw the hunger in my eyes. In his wise heart he knew that he would have to sacrifice his shirt to buy me that toy, which cost twenty rupees. He spent it all on me. When we had returned home, he told my mother that he could manage for a few more months with the shirts he had.

When I held that toy van in my hand, it was like my greatest wish had come true. It felt like I could achieve anything I wanted. My father, with that one simple act, gave me the space to believe that dreams can come true. I carried that toy van everywhere, even when I slept.

He gave me the gift of believing in a different life for myself.

It was not about the amount of money he spent; it was the love that he showed me. When I think of that day, I am so grateful to him. He gave me the gift of believing in a different life for myself. Realizing my hunger for a life of luxury, my father educated me in the values of self-respect, principles, ethics, integrity, and honesty. He knew that by following the path I chose, I could easily be swayed and tempted to lose my way. Those memories and lessons will last forever, and they inspired me to be who I am today.

DISRUPTOR

While my father's impact on me was profound, he is not the only one who shaped who I am today. While that list is actually quite long, one particular story stands out about why I am the way I am.

As a child, I was a disruptor and never took no for an answer. I was an energetic five-year-old and boldly questioned the ways of the world. I was clueless about the disparities in the classes of society. But in India, and often in big cities around the world, the rich and poor do not live in separate neighborhoods; they are just one street away from each other. We lived in the lower middle-class side of Tagore Gardens. Across the road, a stone's throw away, the rich, with their big houses and shiny windows, were clearly visible. There was just one road that divided the rich from the poor, and we were discouraged from crossing to the other side.

I was the youngest of three kids and was always getting into trouble. As a spunky, mischievous kid, I asked my father many questions which all started with "why." "Why can't I cross the road?" "Why don't we have a big house like our neighbor, Mr. Pathak?" My father simply warned me not to venture to the other side of the street. But like many kids, when someone told me not to do something, I did the exact opposite.

My first interaction with Mr. Pathak began when his son returned from London. Mr. Pathak was a friendly fellow. He was always kind to me, perhaps because I was a cute kid who was always happy to chat with the "uncle" across the road. They would call me over and I would be wide-eyed and curious about the son's life in a foreign land. When Mr. Pathak's son was home, he would share wonderful stories about how he traveled by plane, ate different kinds of foods, and he showed me a one-pound note, (this was back when they still had one-pound notes. In 1983, England started converting to the one-pound coin). It amazed me how many rupees could be exchanged for that single note from a faraway country.

I was fascinated by the unfamiliar lifestyle that was just a short distance from my home. My ears would perk up whenever I heard Mr. Pathak's voice. I would run across, wave at him, say something cute, and he would invite me to his front yard and give me a chocolate. One day, I mustered up the courage to ask him if I could see inside his house. From the outside it looked huge and imposing, like a palace. I was burning with curiosity to see what it was like on the inside. Despite my parents' warnings not to mix with the rich people across the road, I still did. But, as I recall it, I was the only one from our humble neighborhood who was welcomed.

Mr. Pathak said he liked the way I was constantly asking questions and let me into his home. It was a three-story house with many rooms and attached bathrooms. I was in awe as I climbed each floor gazing at the pristine walls, furniture, and décor. That entire time I was indoors, I didn't sweat in the summer heat—cool air was part of the luxurious ambience.

Mr. Pathak even offered me a cold drink from his refrigerator (which I had never seen in my life.) It was a cold Coca-Cola—a foreign drink. A rarity. I was bursting with pride; I was the only one who had had the chance to drink a soda. No one from my side of the street would splurge on such an expensive drink. I savored every drop of that icy Coca-Cola.

My visits to Mr. Pathak's house left a huge impact on my understanding of the world. I couldn't imagine why houses that were only one street away were worlds away in size. Mr. Pathak's encouragement also made me bold enough to dare to do what others dared not—crossing the road was just the beginning. And I dared to dream that I could become someone like him.

I wouldn't take no for an answer.

FINAL THOUGHTS

Two weeks after my father had passed away, I travelled to Singapore for an interview with Bloomberg News. I missed my father terribly and recalled his words of wisdom to never forget my roots. Yes, I am grounded by my beginnings; however, being able to adapt is the key to surviving in a competitive environment.

While we do follow a path forward, staying connected with our past and taking pride in our backgrounds is about respecting the values that formed the foundation of our character. The experiences that shape us in childhood are what gives us the incentive to view the world from different perspectives and approach problems in new ways. My father's wisdom and my experiences as a child, put me on the path to a future that most only ever dream about.

A BRIDGE NOT TOO FAR

Chapter 1

SEIZING NEW OPPORTUNITIES

When I was twenty years old, I was an enthusiastic, ambitious young man, ready to take on the world. I began my first job in the hospitality industry. It was at the Indian Tourism Development Corporation (ITDC), a good place to start my career. Starting out as a general trainee, I quickly worked my way up. Soon, I became assistant manager and was then promoted to "Executive Assistant to the Senior Vice-President of the Hotels Division."

It was in that position that I started to really learn about people. As the executive assistant to the senior vice president, other executives would make time to have a cup of tea with me. They would be extremely nice, and even offer to buy me dinner. They wanted to present me with gifts, but I would never take such favors. I recognized early on that they were nice to me simply because of my position, not because of who I was as a person. Loyalty is important to me and I stayed loyal to my boss. That loyalty was repaid in kind. It was a lesson I never forgot—the power of loyalty.

Before resigning, my boss made sure that I was taken care of by ensuring I would have a good position. Normally, transfer letters assign someone to a hotel, and the general manager would then assign you to your department. However, before leaving, my boss got his boss to sign my transfer letter, assigning me to the Frontier Restaurant as the assistant restaurant manager, thus ensuring my position would be secure after he left.

Incidentally, the man who replaced him in his role as the senior vice president offered to keep me on as his assistant. But I declined. He said to me, "It's for your own good." I still remember this incident clearly. I told him, "Sir, I worked for this gentleman. There are people who will speak negatively about him. I won't like it. I have always been loyal to him." The new vice president said he could appreciate that, and as it turned out, I was right. People criticized my former boss.

There is an ancient Indian epic, the Mahabharata, which features many interesting characters who discuss several important values. It is a grand tale with great wisdom that is relevant even today. The Mahabharata shares the realities of human emotions like deceit, cheating, hatred, jealousy, treachery, and revenge. The relevance to my story revolves around one character in particular, Karna. I've always found the character of Karna to be impressive. A man who was an outcaste, treated horribly by many, yet he remained faithful to Duryodhana, a prince, until his death. Karna explained why he was steadfastly loyal: when everyone else discriminated against him for his lower lineage, it was Duryodhana who respected him, gave Karna a piece of land, and made him an honorable prince. Duryodhana respected him when others would not. As a result, Karna turned his back even on his own mother, but remained loyal to the man who treated him with respect. Respect and loyalty go hand in hand.

Loyalty is an important characteristic when it comes to

relationships. I believe that loyalty toward a person, or an organization that stands by you, respects you, and supports you, is key to progress. Loyalty builds trust and that is what people appreciate and value in any relationship.

Loyalty builds trust and that is what people appreciate and value in any relationship.

I trusted and respected my boss at ITDC. I would have been a fool not to put my faith in his recommendation to move on from my current position and I recognized that he was setting me up for an even greater opportunity. Frontier was a very famous restaurant at the time. It was important to seize the moment while I could. And this turned into a great learning experience for me.

Much of what I learned is what you'd expect—aspects of hospitality, customer service, management, etc. But there was another important lesson here. At that time, I began to be targeted by my colleagues. Like any other industry and company, there are politics involved, and my colleagues did not like that I was given that opportunity. Nor did they like that I stayed loyal to my former boss and would not participate in bad-mouthing him. I didn't change my personality. I stayed the same. The reason I'm successful is because I have always been steadfast in following my principles.

FINDING LUXURY

My time at ITDC was an important stepping-stone. It affected my understanding of so many aspects of the hospitality industry.

In many ways, it was an excellent job. The ITDC was in the public sector. It was a government job. Very stable and secure. I was rising in the ranks. However, I began to think about my future. I thought, *If I stay in a government organization, no matter how good I am, my promotion will not be based on merit. My promotion will be based on the time I've spent working.* It wasn't what I wanted. I wanted more. I wanted to get to the top faster. And I wanted to work my way up so I could move overseas. All my life, I had seen in the movies that when you go to Bombay (now known as Mumbai), you are more likely to get the chance to travel overseas. So that's what I decided to do. That was my goal.

In the 1980s, the Veela (name has been changed) was one of the most iconic hotels in India and I wanted to work there. I applied, and when I was accepted, I was overjoyed. For a young aspiring man like me, Bombay was considered the city of dreams. I had definitely been inspired by some of the popular Bollywood movies that depicted the poverty-stricken hero making it big in the city. Indian cinema was quite the influencer on me in those days!

To me, Bombay was the gateway to the world. A gateway to a vibrant energy, where anyone can become rich overnight—if they are lucky enough and work hard enough. I was eager to get to work and excited to accept my first job in the city of dreams. I accepted the position of assistant manager before I left my previous job at ITDC. But I had not informed my family about my switch in jobs until after I accepted the position.

To me, Bombay was the gateway to the world. A gateway to a vibrant energy, where anyone can become rich overnight—if they are lucky enough and work hard enough.

When I told my family, my dad was very upset and disappointed. He admonished me for leaving a secure position in the government. He added that most people would do just about anything to get a government service job, and I was throwing it all away. He didn't understand what I had in mind. This made me even more determined to prove to my father that I had made the right decision.

When I was boarding the train to Bombay, my father said something that I still can recall to this day: "This is the height of immaturity: job-hopping all the time. You do not value money." I understood why he felt that way. My father was in a government job and felt strongly that he had always earned enough and had a level of security that wasn't possible in other jobs. He couldn't see it from my perspective.

His parting remarks were hard to hear. I greatly admired my dad and respected him. But I needed to go anyway. I pleaded with him to see it from my point of view. "I want to see the world. To learn new things." He wasn't able to see it that way. In my father's mind, I was nothing more than a kid. He had no faith that I would rise to the heights I had envisioned for myself. I really wanted to earn his respect and that day, despite his words, I knew that one day he would understand.

THE NEXT CHAPTER

Once I started at the Veela, things rapidly changed. I joined as an Assistant Manager of the Italian restaurant but in just three days, I was asked to be the executive assistant to the managing director! I never could have predicted that. It was a great fit. With him, I learned a great deal about luxury and service. I was only there for a couple years, but it made quite an impact. Yet, I still yearned for more. I wanted to discover the world. I wanted to see and experience new places, and in order to do that, I needed to learn more about the world and explore the hospitality industry in other countries.

I began seeking other opportunities outside of India, specifically in Singapore. My former boss at the ITDC helped me with this endeavor as well. I eventually found a job managing the Bengal Tiger restaurant (name has been changed). I was so excited to be making this next step toward my goal of going overseas. It was part of my plan, however what I didn't foresee was how I was going to exit my job at the hotel. When it came time to resign, the managing director's wife came to me and said "You can't resign! You cannot go. My husband loves you. You do a lot of things for him. Think about it." I said, "No. I don't even have to think about it because this is the chance of a lifetime."

I learned another important lesson at this point in my career—it is important to be able to say no, and it is just as important to say it diplomatically. Months later, the managing director's wife traveled to Singapore and came to the Bengal Tiger restaurant to see me. As we chatted, she said, "Oh, this is small time. I can't believe you left my husband for *this*." She was not happy with me or my decision. I think she felt that I had been disrespectful to her and her husband. I wish I had known how to say "no" more politely or be more diplomatic in resigning from the Veela. I believe she would have been more understanding about why I was moving on. Being able to say no is a really good skill to have, but I still have not changed much in that regard. I am a forthright person by nature.

FINAL THOUGHTS

I am very grateful for those early experiences. They are a large part of my success in life. By working with ITDC, I received an opening in the hospitality industry. It was where I was able to really recognize my dreams, really envision them. What I wanted for myself was very important, even when people said it couldn't be done, or that I shouldn't try because it was too risky. I learned the power of believing in myself in spite of all those challenges. Somehow, I just knew that I would figure it out. I just had to seize every opportunity that came my way and stick to who I was as a person.

ITDC was also my first experience in really learning how to understand people. Throughout the years, being able to relate to people has been important to my success in working with colleagues, with employees, and with the customers themselves. If you don't understand people, you won't get anywhere in business—not just the hospitality business, but in any business.

Likewise, loyalty was another value I learned in the business world. It is not just loyalty to your boss or your company, it is also loyalty to yourself. Loyalty to your dreams. I also learned that when you maintain a high level of loyalty to your principles and to your team, it is often repaid.

There is one final thought I want to leave with you. My time at ITDC and at the Veela helped me realize one other really important factor about my personality: I wanted to innovate and create; therefore, the old school of thought did not work for me. Not for the plans I had for myself, nor for the plans I had for the business. I couldn't play it safe. I couldn't sit back and wait for good things to come to me. I had to seize new opportunities. I needed to learn more, so that I could push the boundaries, or I would never be able to make my dreams a reality. And that was of paramount importance to me. It still is.

Chapter 2

LEARNING CURVES

In the early 1990s, hospitality was recognized as the domain of those from Europe or America, not for Indians. Indeed, India was a very different country back then. It was closed to global trends and products. The country had no malls, department stores, or supermarkets. Overseas products were not available, and locals had no knowledge of other kinds of cuisines. I had never even seen, never mind tasted, broccoli. I assumed that it was just a green cauliflower. My education in India clearly did not have a global approach. So when I travelled out of India for the first time, everything was new: it was my first time on a plane, my first time in a new cultural environment, and I had to adjust to new people and new places.

At twenty-five, I was excited, curious, and, most of all, ambitious. I was very eager to prove my worth. The Bengal Tiger was an Indian restaurant in Singapore. I was geared up for an adventurous journey in a world of hospitality, which I believed was going to bring me into the world of luxury.

No one from my neighborhood back in India had ever left to travel abroad, and here I was working in Singapore. It was a huge deal in those days. My mom thought I was a hero, and she spoke of me with pride to all her friends. My father still didn't really understand what drove me to want these things for my-self, but I think he was proud of me, too.

As the assistant manager of the Bengal Tiger restaurant, I had a steep learning curve ahead of me. I faced criticism and embarrassment due to my poor English-speaking skills. I lacked the polish of an English education, and I would often hesitate to communicate with customers. It was a humbling experience, which motivated me to work harder and develop myself. First of all, I recognized that I really needed to learn English.

Within a few months my English had improved, and I was able to interact with clients with more confidence. Soon, I was talking with many influential customers: bankers, minis-ters, lawyers, etc. In just one year, I was happy with what I had achieved. In a short time, I had created a life for myself. I had learned a new language, developed my personal brand and style, and developed relationships with important people. I felt that I had accomplished more than expected—certainly more than others had expected of me, but even more than I had expected of myself in some ways.

I also came to recognize that people learn in two ways: One is through a formal education; The other is by exposure and experience in the real world. My own education has come pri-marily from experience, and when your education comes from that kind of exposure alone, you start thinking very differently. I craved new and different things to learn. In my current job, I was again starting to feel stifled. There weren't many opportunities for growth anymore with that company. If I had stayed, I knew my career growth would have ended there, as would any oppor-tunities to learn and experience new places. I wanted more.

My ambition was to create something bigger. I wanted to be a part of the world of luxury and glamour, and that just wasn't possible if I stayed at the Bengal Tiger. It was time to make a move and take a step up the career ladder. I started looking for new opportunities.

THE NEXT OPPORTUNITY

Have you ever heard of the "Yellow Car Phenomena?" It's an idea from Lee Colan, the co-founder of the L Group. I'm paraphrasing here, but essentially the idea is that if you make the choice to look for yellow cars, you will start to see them everywhere. Not because there are more of them, but because your mind is focused on them. Before they were background, but once you make them important, your brain pays attention and brings them into focus. Opportunities and success work the same way.[2]

To find new opportunities you need to associate with new people. People who learn through experience need to be opportunity hunters and find the right people to associate with. You need to meet with diverse groups from different cultural backgrounds. When you expand and create a circle of influence, it gives you the ability to hunt for new opportunities. I was on the lookout for other opportunities, and I was actively using my network for this purpose. I focused on it. And like those yellow cars, they quickly appeared. I soon learned of an opening in a restaurant at a five-star luxury hotel. I applied for the position of executive assistant manager (EAM). I was invited for the interview. The interviewer asked many insightful questions which I answered confidently. The interview went well. I showcased my ability and experience, and I knew I was qualified for the job.

2 Lee Colan, "How to Use the Yellow Car Phenomenon," Inc.com (Inc., August 12, 2015), https://www.inc.com/lee-colan/how-to-use-the-yellow-car-phenomenon. html.

Yet, at the end, the interviewer said, "I'm ready to give you the position of a waiter."

I thought, *What!?* I was surprised by his offer, "But I am here for the executive assistant manager (EAM) position." I replied. "I have the experience and knowledge to do this job."

The interviewer looked at me. "That may be so, but you are an Indian man, working as a manager in an Indian restaurant. What is your experience and knowledge worth?" To this day those words ring in my head. I knew I would always have to work twice as hard to prove myself and to overcome the prejudice of others.

"What about my familiarity with all of the rich and influential clientele?" I asked.

He shook his head. "You can do a much better job as a waiter, because you will be actually serving them."

That day, I made a promise to myself that I would be successful in the international arena of hospitality.

I left in a daze, his words ringing in my ears ... "you can start as a waiter" ... "no big deal working in an Indian restaurant" ... That interview really shook me up. It was a wake-up call. My mother thought of me as a hero, but in that moment, I felt like a zero. After some time and some reflection, I realized that part of my journey was to face these obstacles. Not everyone would be helpful. Not everyone would even be fair. This wouldn't be the only setback, nor my only encounter with racism, and I needed to learn to face these issues and overcome them. This incident spurred me forward to find a way to break this cultural stereotyping. I couldn't let it defeat me.

When I shared my interview experience with friends, they

said that I should just accept it, and this is the way the industry worked. It was not going to be easy to climb the ladder of success. I shouldn't feel badly, and I should just stay in my job. That wasn't going to work for me. I wanted better for myself, and even if I had to find a different path to the top, I would do it. That day, I made a promise to myself that I would be successful in the international arena of hospitality. That's when I decided that I would learn and discover more about the industry. I would prove that I had the capability to innovate and create, just like anyone else in the hospitality field.

FINAL THOUGHTS

Failure has been my best teacher. One thing I have discovered is that everyone has dreams to create a new reality. Those who dare to pursue their dreams are the ones that are passionate about learning and improving themselves. They learn how to deal with the world, how to hone their skills to climb up each rung of their career ladder, despite setbacks.

Quite frankly, the catalyst behind my ambition has always been my detractors. They have fueled my ability to push forward and to continue to challenge the status quo. In some cases, my detractors inspired more immediate action, like learning English or dressing a certain way. At the Bengal Tiger, I was often mocked for my cheap clothing in addition to my lack of English. But those were things I could fix. And I did. In fact, I now speak four languages: English, Hindi, German, and Punjabi.

Other detractors presented more complicated issues that took more time to resolve. I knew that I couldn't let that interviewer get me down. I had to present the same energy, enthusiasm, conviction, and confidence that I'd always had in myself if I was going to find the next big opportunity. This was a very important lesson for me. I had to adopt a mindset of "Always be learning."

I really think this is something that is important at every stage in your career. If you ever stop learning, you are dead in the water. And I also learned that racism and stereotyping couldn't stop me if I didn't let them. It might make it harder, and I might have to find alternate paths to my goals, but I couldn't let it stop me. Having that confidence and belief in my own ability to find a solution was one of the greatest takeaways from this time in my life. I couldn't let a few learning curves slow me down. I started looking for other openings. I interviewed for all kinds of jobs, and eventually I was led to an opportunity that would genuinely change the course of my career.

Chapter 3

CREATIVITY AND INNOVATION

A new and shiny opportunity came up in 1994. The Bengal Tiger restaurant was now a huge success, and I was looking for the next step. I had made a bit of a name for myself when I came across an opportunity to head up a new restaurant, and to move to a new city. I was headed to Bangkok.

When I arrived in Bangkok, I instantly felt at home. At that time, Bangkok was like a village. It felt a little like coming home. It was very like India to me. I also had a lot of friends who had also moved to Bangkok from India. So I was very, very happy, and I was also excited about the new job that awaited me.

In one part of the city, there was a complex of condominiums that was newly built. These were large apartments, but no one was interested in buying the property because the location was unpopular. On the street level, there were commercial properties available. One of the owners wanted to create a microbrewery in one of the larger spaces. I was hired as the general manager of the project. We partnered up with a German brand, Bräuhaus which brewed its own in-house beer, all based on techniques and paraphernalia imported from Germany. What was crazy was that I had never had any experience with brewing. It was the first time I'd even heard the word "microbrew." It was the first time I saw how beer is made. It was an amazing experience.

As the general manager, I oversaw the chef and all the staff. It took me some time to really understand German food and beer, but I was really lucky because the staff knew what they were doing. The food was fantastic, and the beer was amazing. In the 600-seat restaurant/brewery we offered a simple bar menu of less than fifteen items and created a fun ambience with a live jazz band. What I really brought to this project was my expertise in marketing, in managing the staff, and in understanding the customer experience.

It took some time to gain popularity. When I opened this restaurant, I said, "No print advertising. Nothing. We'll just do a radio ad." The idea of focusing on radio ads began on my trip from the airport to my job interview with Bräuhaus. I was stuck in traffic. Everybody is stuck in traffic in Bangkok (which has just the worst traffic), and 80 percent are listening to the radio during that time. So I thought, *We can use that.* And I still know this—the telephone number of this restaurant was 6611111. It is forever stuck in my brain. We'd hired a creative ad agency to create a radio ad spot for us. Just a simple advertisement on the radio: "Where are you? I am at 6611111." That's it. That's the entire ad spot. But it attracted curious people. And it was just the start. The marketing got people in the door, but where we really excelled was in our service.

NEW IDEAS IN SERVICE

Our level of service started with our responsiveness to callers from the radio advertisement. Customers now had the phone number memorized, and would call solely out of curiosity. So I hired ten people to man the phones, twenty-four hours a day. We had three shifts of ten people at all times, just for reservations. When people called the number, it would never go to voicemail. Customer calls were answered by a real person and that made all the difference. It all came down to customer experience, and that is something I never forgot.

Many people have asked me why I did that. It seemed risky to most. But I had a gut feeling that the restaurant would become very popular. And I had learned from previous experiences how important it was for customers to have that level of personal service. There were other small things I changed for similar reasons. One of them was the point-of-sale system. I knew the old system would crash under the heavy load of customers, so I anticipated this and upgraded to a better one. I also changed how bartenders poured beer to prevent excess waste. The more precise we could be, the better our revenue and the better the customer experience.

Our goal was to ensure that customers were getting the right attention. The staff was available immediately to take their orders. I timed their efficiency. On average, in any other bar it would take about five minutes to order a second drink. In ours, not a minute was wasted.

Normally, a dining establishment of our size would have sixty staff members—we had 120. Additionally, we had fifty people taking care of the whole cleaning process. With over 170 staff members, we made sure the customers did not have to wait for anything.

Our servers also did not clean; they were focused on customer service. We had a separate cleaning crew for clearing and cleaning tables. This workflow enabled waiting customers to be seated in the shortest possible time. And while people were waiting outside, our staff would take orders so that when they were seated, they wouldn't have to wait for their drinks.

I also wanted to make sure the restaurant had the right ambience. We added a little international flair with a fantastic jazz band. Our menu of food and drinks was top notch, and our staff created a very lively atmosphere. We had upped our service and that led to greater success in the long run. We reached a stage where we had about 800 people waiting patiently to enter the restaurant. At that time, one US dollar was equivalent to twenty-five Thai bahts, and Bräuhaus's revenue was US$4 million a year. The most exciting byproduct of our success was that not only did the restaurant make money, but also that all the condominiums, which were previously unpopular, suddenly became hot buys. The location became so trendy that the street Sukhumvit Soi 24, today, has over a hundred restaurants.

SUCCESS

The microbrewery's success was a great lesson in my journey. My approach was to run the business sensibly with a service-oriented concept. I had an efficient team in place. I also hired a very enterprising lady as my assistant. Her English wasn't that great, but she had the right energy to learn and manage the staff. This was very important to me. Anyone can learn a language, but having the right energy is something that can't be taught. I paid for her English lessons. I invested in her because I believed in her, and if you have great people working for you, you want to keep them working for you by giving them the support and resources they need to be successful.

This was the first time I could really hire the people I wanted, based solely on my own criteria. I decided I wanted to look for passion. I wanted somebody whose thought process was 10 to 15 percent similar to mine. Why not 100 percent, you might ask? Because I value other perspectives, too. I wanted someone who could understand what I was thinking, but also someone who could provide additional value—provide their own opinions with creative solutions for the customer experience. Most of all, I wanted someone with the right energy who *wanted* to be there. It is always a team effort. I really learned how important hiring the right type of people is to a business's success, and it's something that I would implement again later on in my career, and to even greater extents.

> *My strength was in having the creativity*
> *to innovate, and if I had the freedom to create,*
> *it would lead to success.*

Innovation, even in staffing decisions, has been a key to my success. I focused on innovating new ideas based around every aspect of the customer's experience, and the success that decision led to confirmed something for me: my strength was in having the creativity to innovate, and if I had the freedom to create, it would lead to great rewards.

FINAL THOUGHTS

Working at Bräuhaus was a transformational experience. In the microbrewery business, there was a lot of leeway for me to explore my ideas and apply them. It was the first time I had truly had the freedom to implement my ideas in a big way. I could be creative, I could innovate, and I could trust my instincts. I stayed on with the company and opened a second location back in Singapore. The new location did very well, too. By that point, I was now the Director of Business Development. I am so grateful for my time with this company. It was on Sukhumvit Soi 24, that bustling street, that I discovered my strengths and discovered my potential.

Then the company wanted me to open a third location in an area where I knew it would not work. When I visited the prospective site, I could read the people there. It wasn't the right place for it. Starting way back at ITDC, I had cultivated the skill of watching people and understanding them. This skill came into play here. I just had a gut feeling. I refused. I said, "This will never work. This will bring the whole company down."

Unfortunately, they said I had to do it. I ran the projections, and they were also negative. I did not want to start a new location, so I knew it was time to move on. I had gotten all I could out of the experience, and they were starting to focus on maintaining the status quo rather than innovating and trusting my instincts. I was quickly headhunted by Smokin' Nachos (name has been changed); they were looking to expand into Indonesia, and they offered to send me to the US for training. It was an amazing opportunity that came to me at just the right time.

Chapter 4

THE SHINE OF
A MENTOR

Going to the Unites States for a training program with Smokin' Nachos was both exhilarating and intimidating. I had always wanted to live in the US, and I was excited to work for a well-known international company. I knew there would be a lot I could learn from them, but I never imagined I would ever get the kind of education I received. This would be the foundation that would lay the groundwork for my greatest successes that were yet to come. I knew I had talents, skills, and the potential to do so much more. Luckily, hindsight is 20/20 and I can now recognize this perfect opportunity for what it was.

At Smokin' Nachos, I was an apprentice to the US-based head of operations, Joe Santiani (name has been changed). Honestly, I didn't know what to expect when I took the job. I thought I'd had adequate training in both hospitality and in restaurants. However, what Santiani did was open my mind to something more. He was the one to sharpen my skills. There were many tangible gaps in my knowledge of being a restaurateur, and these gaps were filled while I trained under his sharp and vigilant eye. It was under his guidance that I learned that it is only when we apply our knowledge of the outside world to the workplace that we discover our weaknesses.

Only when we apply our knowledge of the outside world to the workplace that we discover our weaknesses.

My time in the US was the grounding I needed to stand tall and proud amongst those who were seasoned and well-known. In fact, I can openly say that much of the nitty-gritty trade secrets of hospitality I know today were gleaned from that experience. I refer to Santiani as my godfather with much fondness, and I still value his advice and friendship today. I fondly recall the eighteen months of training I had under him, and I consider him a great teacher and a restaurant guru. Working with him was a reality check and it made me realize my own arrogance and ignorance.

I first met Santiani in Singapore a year or two prior to this, in 1994. That was during my very first trip outside of India, when I was still struggling to fit in and figure out how to communicate better. When Santiani interviewed me, he must have noticed the fire in my eyes and the burning ambition in my heart. It was a year later that he and his company recruited me and accepted me into their training program.

Feeling slightly intimidated and unsure of myself, I didn't know how I would manage. My English-speaking skills were still not as good as they could have been, and I was unfamiliar with American culture. Despite all these doubts, I was determined to make the most of this apprenticeship. It was the best decision of my life.

On our career paths, we sometimes meet certain people who create a deep impression and at the same time transform our way of thinking. You could say that Joe Santiani was one such person to me. He was a kind, gentle soul, but a hard taskmaster. About a decade older than me, with a thick American accent, Santiani had piercing blue eyes that missed nothing, and a demeanor that was both disciplined and friendly. He was the chisel that refined my rough edges.

Even today, I appreciate him for all his teachings. Joe Santiani, head of operations was like my Yoda, the Jedi Master. He didn't hesitate to test my knowledge, or rather my ignorance. Not yet in my thirties, I was already fiercely motivated to make it big, but I had my weaknesses. I was overly impatient and overly confident. Santiani was the one who steered my mind toward a deeper understanding of the service industry. His lessons were necessary. He taught me that the devil is in the details—something I've never forgotten.

HANDS-ON TRAINING

It was the start of an intense period of training. Santiani's method of teaching was very hands-on and time-consuming. You could say it was a test in patience. In the first week training under him, we started with the unit review process. This was a grueling inspection of each of the restaurant's franchises. We would go through bags of wet and dry garbage, inspecting the contents. At each outlet, a lot can be gleaned from the contents of a garbage bag: whether the quality of food is below par, there is pilferage, the amount of waste, or any other issues. We were like detectives, wearing gloves, as we rummaged through the smelly refuse. This inspection took place at three-thirty in the morning, when no one was around, and we could deduce the possibilities from all the evidence.

After completing our garbage review, we would then go and sit at a twenty-four-hour diner, have some coffee and pie, and wait for the restaurant to open. Later, at around 7:00 a.m., when the morning team arrived, it was time to examine the kitchen. Everything was scrutinized carefully there, too. The freezer, dry storage, product expiration dates, and cleanliness and hygiene were all meticulously studied and assessed.

As an example of our routine, we took a flight to Cincinnati, landed around 5:00 p.m., and got our rental cars to drive to a local chain hotel. Santiani never informed a restaurant that we were coming. That evening we would go to a competitor's restaurant to try to understand what ours was lacking in that market. We would dine, but Santiani's antenna was on alert to compare the best practices. At times, Santiani would study the psychology of the diners. From their body language, he would accurately guess what they would order. And he was always right!

That's how we spent our first evening. We enjoyed our dinner without any alcohol because we knew that the following day we had to be up early to check the garbage. When we were at the restaurant franchise, we didn't just check the interior; the exterior was equally important. Before going through the bins, we would walk around the stand-alone restaurant. It was important that there was no grease in the back area. That was usually the delivery location, and before it was taken into the kitchen, much of the produce would be sitting outside where there could be a risk of cross contamination. There was a special type of paper we used to test for grease. We would slide it near the door of the kitchen to check for any grease. Another wet white paper was placed on the road to check how much blackness would be there. This sheet of paper would be sent to the lab to check if it was grease or something else.

All the exhaust vents were inspected and in addition to the hygiene check, all produce were screened to ensure they follow the Hazard Analysis Critical Control Point (HACCP) guidelines. It was a rigid process—there were no cutting corners or taking the word of the manager. Everything had to be checked firsthand. Each unit was reviewed with precision. Santiani—I have to give him credit for this—didn't find this process tedious or boring. Day in and day out, he followed this routine with a passion. Doing the same thing every single day and not getting bored is an achievement in itself. I greatly admired this about him, and it is something I try to emulate to a degree to this day.

In America, iced tea, coffee, and sodas are common beverages usually served at all dining establishments. Other than the coffee, iced tea is dispensed through a large container and sodas through a fountain. When we followed our inspection routine, the nozzles for both of these dispensaries were opened and inspected to check for cleanliness. Coffee machines can get filthy if left unchecked; that, too, was dismantled and inspected. The dishwasher rollers were swept with white paper to check whether they were clean.

Each kitchen appliance had a temperature gauge, but they were usually inaccurate, so we brought our own thermometer. When we inspected the coffee machines, the temperature was first checked with our own thermometer, and then the cleanliness of the filters and other parts were checked. A temperature check is also done with the deep fryer. The oil was also inspected, and if it was "broken", meaning it had lost its viscosity, it was either disposed of or sent to the company for recycling. Ninety percent of the time these unit reviews would receive a failing grade. This kept the managers humble and constantly vigilant to maintain their standards. A smelly glass, a bitter cup of coffee, a soggy french fry, all of these are caused by the equipment in the kitchen.

I learned quite a few trade secrets from Santiani, which I still apply today. For example, the crispness of iceberg lettuce lasts a maximum of eighteen hours. The moment the produce is received, we ensure the temperature is maintained to preserve its freshness. This type of detail makes a difference in service excellence and creates the reputation of a restaurant. I learned that many small issues could lead to bigger issues where a customer ends up feeling disappointed, especially if the service or hygiene is not up to par.

PHILOSOPHICAL TRAINING

Besides the hands-on teachings, it was Santiani's wisdom that had a profound effect on me. He would say that no job is too small. To become big, one must be able to understand the small jobs. Small changes bring about big differences. To quality-check kitchen equipment, one must first know how to use the equipment, and what the equipment provides. To this day, I am well-versed in how to work a coffee machine. I can prepare a perfect cup and I know if there is a problem with the machine.

Santiani did not avoid grunt work. "At no point should you shy away from putting your hands in garbage," he told me. Putting his statement into practice, he would even mop the floors to show the restaurant staff how it was supposed to be done. The unit reviews often took three days to complete. We started with the garbage bags, but then checked the food delivery trucks to see that the supplies were meeting the correct standards of quality. There were times that we would check the local produce from the starting point of its journey to ensure quality and consistency. It was a non-stop review process.

I realized Santiani's every action was a lesson in humility. Back then, there was not much talk about diversity, not like there is today. Yet even then Joe Santiani was an example for others on the subject. He taught me the biggest lesson of my life—self-respect comes from respecting others; it is a two-way street. My mentor's behavior showed me that no one is inferior; respect is given to those who deserve it, and to those who have talent and skill. Diversity, equity, and inclusion (DE&I) were yet to be used as the buzzwords in the corporate world, but at a time in my life where I was still being judged based on my race, my lack of formal education, and other things unrelated to my abilities and success, Santiani made it clear that he believed that success isn't based on the color of one's skin, nor one's background. Success is based on an individual's traits and attitudes. I had carried an inferiority complex like a weight around my neck for a long time, but my sense of inferiority disappeared when I worked with him.

He taught me the biggest lesson of my life—
self-respect comes from respecting others;
it is a two-way street.

My mentor set an example on how to motivate and inspire. He proved himself time and again—well-dressed and head of his division, yet he rolled up his sleeves to rummage through garbage. There was a moment when I asked myself: *Is this what I signed up for in my career?* Going through bins in the middle of the night? I had never expected that this was part of the job description. I had chosen my path in the hospitality industry with the impression that I would be sitting in a prestigious office, with a team to assist me, having interactions with corporate bigwigs and entrepreneurs. But Santiani taught me that if we want to succeed in any task, big or small, one must be willing to know how to do it, and to do it with sincerity and passion.

I was empowered by his behavior and the example he set. I discovered more about my values, skills, and capacity. There was a time when I worked as a dishwasher. It was a necessity at the time. Here, in the US, putting my hands in the garbage was not a necessity for me, but it was to understand that there is dignity in every task that leads to growth. It is a symbolic action that taught me that if we are to be the best at what we do, we must feel that no job is below our dignity, and the dignity of labor exists in every area of hospitality. Whether you are a dishwasher or a kitchen assistant, you can learn something and move forward in life.

If I was on a quest for self-respect, I could not have the attitude that getting my hands dirty was below me. Even today, I have never forgotten the wisdom of Joe Santiani's teachings.

I could not have the attitude that
getting my hands dirty was below me.

Today, when many think that I am about to retire, I have instead pursued a direction to teach hospitality. My life goal has always been to make every customer experience more meaningful and memorable. Now my goal is to teach the message to the next generation, just as my mentor once taught me.

When I think of my mentor, Santiani, he didn't blink at my position or at the color of my skin. I remember when I first met him. It was when I landed at the Orlando airport. After a twenty-hour flight, a bit dazed and intimidated, I entered the US for the first time, and I saw him waiting for me. I was exhausted, nervous, and unsure of what to expect, but Santiani was there to pick me up. I was surprised to see him. Being a senior level executive, I thought he would send some employee. Most people would have sent an assistant or a chauffeur. Many wouldn't have sent anyone at all and left it up to me to find my own transportation. But he came personally to meet me; he didn't even think twice about it. Santiani led me to a car rental and rented a Volvo for me. (I had to adapt quickly to driving on the left-hand side.) I followed his car to a luxury complex, where he had arranged an apartment for me. For a senior executive to take time out of his busy day for an intern meant a lot. I was in awe of him from then on.

A NEW EDUCATION

As Santiani's apprentice, I visited around thirty-five different cities and covered over a hundred restaurants. But I was still ignorant about wines, certain foods, sauces, etc. Santiani would test me often, especially when I was learning to refine my taste buds. He put my taste sensors through wines, sauces, meats, herbs, salads, and different cuisines. He would explain in detail the difference between fine dining and casual dining. When we would eat at different restaurants, he would discuss each item on the menu, and critically examine whatever we ordered.

At times, he would test my taste in wines. He would trick me with a glass of cheap wine and call it expensive. Initially, I was eager to please, and agreed with him. Later, I became more discerning—and more honest—and told him what I really thought. Making mistakes taught me more than trying to impress him did. He would laugh when I was trying to show off that I was becoming more knowledgeable, but he was the smarter man. I finally understood that I didn't have to impress him, I had to go with what I felt was right. And that is where I really started developing my sense of self-respect and confidence. People tend to do things to impress others, but it is when you do things for yourself that you will become great.

---

*People tend to do things to impress others,
but it is when you do things for yourself
that you will become great.*

Besides the little nuggets of wisdom he imparted, I also met and made friends with chefs and other restaurateurs. I was given the opportunity to create my first concept dish with the chef of one of our well-known restaurants in Maryland and Washington, DC. It was a pasta dish: penne arabiatta with vodka broth and red pepper corn. We worked on this dish for a month before it rolled out in all of the restaurants in that chain. I was so proud and happy to see that diners enjoyed my creation. I found I had a passion for cooking and for trying out new ideas. I love to recreate some of the Italian dishes from those restaurants' menus. Even today, I can cook many of them from memory.

WORKING IN THE U.S.

Later, I moved to Dallas from Orlando, and began working at the company headquarters. In Dallas, my new home was spacious from my perspective. It was a beautiful two-bedroom apartment with a brilliant view of a golf course. I would tell my mother that my home had a wide expansive view of greenery. She was impressed and happy for me. On weekends, I would explore the state. I'd drive to San Antonio, near the border of Mexico. Other times I would drive to Austin, or other places.

I was relishing my time in the U.S., and I enjoyed my work. Santiani had taught me how to better manage a team, how to prepare excel spreadsheets, how to select a suitable site for a restaurant, and he taught me a lot more about customer psychology. It was something that already interested me; I had made a study of it at my previous positions as well. It was a foundational aspect of my success at Bräuhaus. But this training took the idea of customer experience to new heights.

It was a beautiful life, but a lonely one. I had no partner to share it with. My life, as perfect as it was, didn't fill my heart with joy. Looking back, I am absolutely sure that if my wife Anita had been with me then, I would have stayed and settled in the U.S. But without family and friends, I wasn't happy. Not really. Santiani had nominated me for the position of International Director of Operations, and personally asked me to stay on with the company. But deep down, I knew that my restless spirit would demand a change. I needed a different kind of environment and I knew that I would find it closer to home, in some part of Asia.

I took with me all of Santiani's teachings: He taught me that our efforts are never in vain; even the smallest efforts are important in the journey to becoming perfect. There are no shortcuts to success. By doing the smallest tasks consistently, one is filled with the power of confidence. The change he inspired in me has enabled me to share those very lessons with others. That was really his goal; he believed that we could create a domino effect of transformation. When people cross our paths, we learn from them *and* we teach them. This kind of transference and interactional knowledge can benefit all of humanity. It is one reason I am so confident that the lessons I am sharing throughout this book can be applied to any business, not just the hospitality industry.

FINAL THOUGHTS

My time in the US with Santiani was a turning point in my life. My training there, even today, gave me the ability to lead my team because I know each person's job; I have been in their shoes. I can still open any dishwashing machine and clean it and tell them how it is to be done. I teach the staff how to check the temperature. The trainees at my company are often amazed. First of all, they don't expect the boss to have a hands-on approach, and they don't expect the boss to have such in-depth knowledge of kitchen appliances. Their respect increases when they see that I can still open any soda machine and tell them what is wrong with it. I can explain a problem with a coffee machine with a single sip of brew.

We often feel that the simple acts and mundane tasks are a waste of time. When I started my training, it seemed ridiculous to go through garbage bags. I was an aspiring entrepreneur with my head in the clouds. But there is wisdom in these simple acts. Little things in life matter, and if I cannot do the simple things right, I would not be able to handle the complicated ones correctly either. Those small tasks, done perfectly, makes us better at what we do; it leads us to the next task, and so on and so on. By dealing with small tasks, over a period of time, when we add them up, they become a whole project. This vital teaching by Santiani enabled me to handle big projects that were challenging later on in my career. I still divide my projects into small tasks, which then gives me the confidence and motivation to move forward. When we are facing big projects, by dividing them into small and achievable tasks, it becomes easier to focus on the job at hand.

Focusing on the simple, teaches us discipline, consistency, and the right service attitude. These small tasks have taught me how to operate in luxury hospitality, how to understand consumer behavior, and how to motivate my team to believe in me. When I see success from my efforts, I mentally thank Joe Santiani. He gave me the gift of a lifetime. His lessons have taught me the real importance of hospitality and much of his wisdom applies to life as well.

While this training from my mentor has made an impact on me, applying it to the next segment of my life was a different story. Despite his example of remaining humble, I had yet to learn how to rein in my arrogance and the desire to be an accomplished restaurateur. I was overly eager to prove my worth. I thought I knew it all, and when the opportunity to invest in a business came, I jumped in with both feet without checking if the water was warm. Turns out, that would be one of my biggest mistakes, and biggest lessons, of my life.

Chapter 5

BOLD IS GOLD

Working at Smokin' Nachos further reinforced that I was better off in a situation where I had the freedom to be innovative and implement fresh ideas. It's hard to do that in a rigid corporate structure. So, one day, a lady who owned an Indonesian chain of restaurants came to me with an offer. She wanted to expand. She said to me, "We are not doing so well. Can you help us?" It seemed like the perfect opportunity. It was a chance for me to invest in a business and become a partner, not just an employee. I left Smokin' Nachos and I went with her. I had some money saved up, so I put that into the company. Under the agreement, they were supposed to pay me a salary for managing the restaurants, and I would also receive revenue from my share of the business. It seemed like the perfect deal for me. I was filled with enthusiasm, creativity, and the motivation to explore how to build the business.

I implemented my ideas almost immediately. Of course, I started with the same philosophy I used back at Bräuhaus—focus on the customer experience. Excellent service was of the highest priority. I introduced new concepts, and also an innovative cooking technique. As I mentioned before, I found I had a passion for cooking. I created a recipe for a white-coal smoked fish dish. We used white coal because it creates less smoke and is more environmentally friendly. It also added a completely different flavor. It became one of our most popular dishes. Every table seemed to be ordering it. It became a huge trend.

Another change I made was to hire college students from La Roche, Switzerland, and other international students. They were highly trained and highly intelligent servers. People just couldn't believe that for lunch of $60 or $80 Singapore dollars, you could get that level of service. The food was cooked and served very fast. I also stopped offering takeaway service. If people wanted our food, they had to dine at the restaurant.

That recipe and the other changes I implemented were working and kept customers coming back regularly. The business grew exponentially. Soon we had not just two restaurants, but five across Singapore!

I was coming up with many ideas to build on our success. We had created a buzz in the city. I gained confidence in exploring the levels of hospitality service and everything was going great. Until it wasn't. . . .

Don't get me wrong, the restaurants were all doing well. So why did it fall apart? In some ways I still wonder the same thing. Looking back, I think it comes down to one thing: my partners no longer trusted me. Not because I had done anything wrong. More that I was a victim of my own success. My partners thought I was going to take over the business. They ousted me instead. I was left high and dry. I had nothing left. How, you might ask? Well, one lesson everyone should learn from this is to never trust handshake deals and vague verbal promises. Get everything in writing and read those contracts carefully for clauses that can be used against you, like mine was against me. I made the mistake of trusting my partners too much and expecting that trust would be reciprocated. That didn't happen and with nothing else to rely on, there was nothing I could do. I literally lost everything. This bitter lesson, though hard to digest, was key to my development in how I interacted with people.

Looking back, I discovered so much richness in what I had learned and achieved, even in this failure. I learned that I should not trust blindly. A key lesson of human behavior that I uncovered was to interact in a way that doesn't make others feel insecure. Sometimes the lessons from our past become our guiding force. They are like warning signals to think deeply before committing to people or ventures. Understanding one's own weaknesses and strengths gives us an advantage so that we can then make conscious decisions. And how does one learn? Through one's mistakes. Failure is our greatest teacher.

Failure is our greatest teacher.

We often curse ourselves for making mistakes, but we shouldn't. Instead, we should consider them to be opportunities. These are vital practical experiences that help us grow and understand how to function in new environments. I wouldn't have known my fullest potential if I hadn't taken risks and made mistakes. By doing what I did, I became street-smart and willing to explore new areas with confidence. I was not bookish like other executives. I was more of a people-person, curious about the way the world functioned and how businesses thrived. Book knowledge is relevant, but what you learn out in the real world, facing obstacles, is what makes the biggest difference in your life.

THE FULL STORY

Living in a sprawling bungalow in the plush area of Upper Bukit Timah in Singapore, I felt a sense of pride in my achievements as a restaurateur. My life was liberal and lavish. I did not hide being rich. I had a big, fancy house. I had an expensive car. I loved the whole idea of living life to the fullest and spending like there was no tomorrow. I had many friends and was carefree and indulged in every sense of the word. Whiskey, women, and work were my passions. I felt like I could achieve anything—the sky was the limit. I had grand dreams and grander plans. I had my career all planned out. My destiny was in my hands and the world was my oyster. This kind of lifestyle went on for almost two years.

On that last day, I was wearing my tailor-fitted suit, ready for work. I grabbed my briefcase and headed toward my garage where my prized possession, a white Mercedes CLK convertible, was waiting for me. I paused momentarily, mesmerized by the sun's rays sparkling like diamonds on the surface of the pool. My immediate thought was: "Should I drive to Kuala Lumpur in my car or take the shuttle flight . . . ," I decided on the shuttle flight. I called for a cab. It arrived in minutes, and I settled comfortably in the air-conditioned car. The drive was smooth as I gazed out at the lush greenery that lined the highway to the airport. On board the flight, and wherever I went, people greeted me by name and bowed with respect. They wanted to make sure I was getting the best service.

When I returned to Singapore after that trip, I was looking forward to an evening of relaxation with a single malt whiskey. Instead, when I got home it was as if someone had dropped a bomb on everything I loved. I had lost everything: my beloved car, my beautiful house, and millions worth of investment. I was still trying to register that this wasn't all a nightmare, and I would wake up realizing that I was still living the high life. But the padlock on the gate to my home was enough evidence to show me that I had to face the harsh truth. I called up the friend who had encouraged me to invest millions in this venture, but he was not supportive. It was not what I'd expected at all.

The flaw in my character was that when I trusted someone, I tended to trust completely, blindly, and foolishly. In my youthful haste, I invested in what I thought was a potentially successful business opportunity. But then I was betrayed. I had nothing. All I had to my name, was well, my name. I called friends, but they were fair-weather friends. I called people who had said, "Call me anytime day or night," people who I had helped with gifts and favors, but they offered me nothing but empty words. Overnight, my lavish lifestyle faded to nothing.

I fought back the bitterness of regret. Then anger overtook my senses; I was furious. I wanted to lash out at someone. Instead, I curbed my fury and focused on what to do next. I decided I would get the best lawyer and file a case. Unfortunately, I was at a disadvantage there as well. When I had first arrived in Singapore, many well-wishers had advised me to apply for permanent resident status. I never got around to applying, though it would have helped in my current situation.

Since I was not a permanent resident, I would have had to deposit the equivalent of millions of dollars with the court. By that point, I didn't even have enough to last me the next day. I applied for over three hundred jobs, hoping I could start earning some money quickly. It was a daily routine: wake up, look for a job, return home dejected. Even though I got to the interview stage many times, I was either overqualified or not qualified enough. In fact, jobs were hard to come by in those days. It was 1998, and the world economy was in doldrums. I reflected on my upside-down life. My savings were dwindling. I couldn't even afford my favorite freshly brewed coffee. I was getting my daily brew from a polybag which cost only a few cents. I felt a multitude of emotions, from regret to shame to anger. I admitted to myself that I was not going to last much longer with my minimal funds. There was really only one option left.

My only way to rebuild my life was to go back to my roots. I had to return to India, to my home. The thought of facing my family penniless was agonizing. With a heavy heart, I gave away what little I had left for free and managed to get an economy class ticket to Delhi.

On the flight, I was mentally rehearsing what I would say to my family, how I would explain my failure. But no matter how many excuses and reasons I thought of, there was nothing to do but face the truth. It was my failure, and I had to take accountability for my mistakes. I knew, even then, that for the next step, facing this was going to be important. I hadn't done enough research to check if the investment was worthy or not, nor checked if my partners were honorable, and I hadn't protected myself legally. Lesson learned.

RETURNING HOME

It took a lot of guts for me to stand in front of my father. At age thirty, I thought I would be rich, successful, and at the top of my game. And I had been, for a fleeting moment. I thought I knew enough and was ready for the big leagues. Instead, I returned with head bowed, facing my father and a feeling of *How could this happen to me?*

Looking back, my failure in Singapore was the result of my arrogance. What I lacked was humility. I had forgotten my mentor Santiani's most crucial teaching of all—humility. He had been crafting not just my skill set, but my mindset, too. I had been impatient, and to put it mildly, overconfident.

From India to Singapore to Bangkok, and then an internship in America, I felt that I had it all figured out; I knew the tricks of the trade. It's not easy recognizing failures in yourself. I'd had my moments of self-doubt, but it had never occurred to me that I wouldn't be able to make things work out in the end. This was the first time that I was starting to question myself. But it also made me question others in a way I never had before. This life lesson has stuck with me: do not trust anyone blindly. I have learned to be selective with whom I have dealings, and I choose my friends very carefully now.

Standing there, in front of a man I loved and respected and the one person I looked up to with admiration, brought me to the naked truth that I had failed. And failed miserably. I could do nothing to salvage it. I admitted to my father that I had lost everything. He looked at me with a solemn expression.

My mother braced for an outburst, and my siblings were in their rooms with their ears to the door. Standing there in the living room, I sensed the calm before the storm. I prepared for my father's wrath, prepared for his critical remarks, calling me a child and immature as he had done for years. He loved me—I knew that—but respect? That was yet to be earned.

I distinctly remember that day, twenty-two years ago. I could hear the whirring of the fan, *whip-whip-whip*, beads of perspiration popped on my forehead. I felt like I was melting under the heat of my father's gaze. My mother was about to say something. Pre-empting whatever she would whisper in my defense, my dad raised his hand to stop her. She fell silent.

I stood my ground. I was prepared for his rightful indignation and his words which would no doubt knock some sense into me. I had no defense, no excuses. In a calm tone, my father asked me to explain what happened. I did. But I also promised that I would work harder and earn back all that I had lost.

He looked at me and I saw a softening in his expression, he said: "Now I am proud to say you are my son. You have grown up. You have faced the real world. You are still standing tall. Most people would have given up. You have not given up. And you are willing to admit failure. You are no longer a child; you are a man now."

I remember gaping at him. This was the opposite of what I expected. My mother held back tears. Then I understood the deeper reason behind his encouraging words. He, too, had faced highs and lows in his life. His words came from a place of lived experience. My father was a man wise beyond his years. In his heyday, he had enjoyed the heights of comforts and riches, and then suddenly faced street-level poverty.

MY FATHER'S STORY

It all started before 1945, when my grandfather was a well-respected and wealthy man in Punjab. He had dealings with China and had a prosperous business. He had all the luxuries of someone from that era: status, cars, horses, and plenty of cash. My father and his brother were blessed with all the comforts that life had to offer.

Around that time, China was going through a civil war which eventually brought about the worst inflation in the country's history. On the foreign-exchange market, the value of China's money dropped like a dead weight. Overnight, the currency became worthless. My grandfather died penniless, and my father and his brother ended up on the street.

Teaming up with three good friends, the five men did their best to make ends meet. They enrolled in night school and worked during the day to earn a daily wage. My father and uncle worked as peons. My uncle eventually joined the Indian Police Service (IPS). My father joined the Revenue Department and worked as an Income Tax officer.

One of their friends, Sampooran Singh, worked odd jobs before he became famous in Bollywood as Gulzar, the poet and lyricist. His other friend, Tarlochan Singh, sold clothes on the sidewalk. He is now the well-known and successful owner of Brightways Garments Emporium in Karol Bagh. Finally, their third friend, Harbhajan Singh, worked at a construction site and is now considered one of the most prominent builders in Delhi.

That's the kind of life my father had experienced. When he said that I had grown up to face my failures, he believed that I would struggle but still be able to achieve greatness. He knew that the hard knocks of life were necessary lessons, just as it is necessary to cut and polish a rough diamond.

He knew that the hard knocks of life were necessary lessons, just as it is necessary to cut and polish a rough diamond.

My father had lived comfortably, and then faced dire circumstances. The five friends with humble beginnings had faced hardships, like when they would share one glass of milk to sustain themselves. That was the kind of never-give-up attitude that he believed in, and that's what my father finally saw in me.

MOVING ON FROM FAILURE

For me, earning my father's respect and trust was the greatest moment in my life, even in the midst of my failure. In retrospect,

I would say that was the turning point. My father's words empowered me, and there was no looking back after that. Being with my family was a comfort. Yet I sorely missed my luxurious lifestyle. I had tasted the sweet life and I wanted it all back and more. It wasn't greed that spurred me. It wasn't the money, but the sense of ambition. I wanted to experience that feeling—that I had worked hard and became successful from it. When I was abroad, I had taken for granted the perks of being able to spend without a second thought. In India, every cent mattered.

The lifestyle at home and in the neighborhood was exactly the same as I recalled from my childhood. Everyone in the community seemed content, complacent even. Being in that environment was killing my ambition. I wanted to do more, be more. While I was in my father's two-bedroom flat in Sarita Vihar, suffering in the heat, I missed the constant coolness of an air-conditioned environment. I began to feel renewed energy to get back on my feet and look for opportunities elsewhere. I knew in my restless heart that I couldn't settle for just a mediocre existence.

Sitting there, jobless and with no particular idea what to do next, my father came up with a solution to help me out of my rut. He offered to sell his home and move to Dehra Dun, a small town over 1000 kilometers from New Delhi. He suggested opening a shop there, a small outlet to sell Indian nut sweets and milk cakes. By selling his house, he could afford to buy both a small home in Dehra Dun and a sweet shop. This was an incredibly kind offer and would have been a great sacrifice for him and the whole family. I imagined myself sitting at the sales counter, collecting money from the customers, while swatting flies. But I knew in my heart that I wasn't interested in becoming a *halwai*, an Indian sweet-seller. I wanted to get back into the high life of hospitality. That was my calling, my passion, where I believed I would make a difference. What was stopping me? I realized the only thing that was stopping me was me, myself. Nobody else. I thanked my father for his generous offer, but I could not accept it. Instead, I focused on how to get back to the path I'd planned for my life.

FINAL THOUGHTS

And so I once again cast out for new opportunities. As luck would have it, I was offered a very lucrative opportunity to work for the cruise lines with a monthly salary of US$8,000. I just couldn't say no. I returned to Singapore and took the job. At least it was something. It was not a challenging position, but it came with perks. I wasn't sure about the growth opportunities there or the employee culture, but for the moment, that didn't really matter to me. I needed the money. I knew we were there to provide service to the passengers, but it was not necessary to improvise or innovate. It was clearly a mind-numbing job that only required following orders. I also quickly realized that the culture on the cruise ship was very open, and I didn't really like it. There were too many temptations, and much of the crew were more concerned about which person they would be dating that night and getting drunk. Sadly, many shifted into alcoholism. I was worried I would be tempted to do the same if I stayed too long. Ultimately, it was not the job for me.

Building a reputation based on my work ethic, innovation, and creativity in the service industry was how I wanted to achieve my goals. It had to be on my own terms, or not at all. After a month in the job, I resigned and returned home to Delhi. Everyone said I was a fool to give up such a high-paying salary. I believed differently. I would start fresh, and I would earn it all back. I had conviction.

Despite the naysayers, I was focused on what I wanted to do. My experiences in Singapore meeting different people while working in the restaurant and my training period in the US had given me insights on how customer service can be done differently. I enjoy talking to people and learning what they look forward to in life. Developing rapport with others comes naturally to me. These are all traits and skills to which I credit much of my success. Through my interactions with people from different cultures and countries, an idea was brewing in my head. I was keen on getting back into the restaurant and hotel business. It was a bold move, but sometimes bold is where you find the gold.

Chapter 6

REBUILDING ONE STEP AT A TIME

It was 1998, and I left home again to return to the fabulous, vibrant city of Bombay (Mumbai) to start work at the luxury hotel company, the Raj Group (name has been changed). This was a good opportunity for me, and I went into it with my eyes open. This was a good job with an established brand that was known for providing a great experience in India and for its charity work. It was my entry back into the hospitality industry and would be the first step in rebuilding my career. However, I also knew that working for a big corporation like this had both benefits and drawbacks.

The benefits were obvious: good salary, good company, a re-entry to the industry, and a chance to rebuild my reputation. The drawbacks were that, just like I had learned at Smokin' Nachos, working for a big, rigid corporation meant innovation and creativity would be stifled. There is more red tape in a company like this. While getting back to the level of leadership that allowed me to be creative was important, for now I knew this was the right move.

Just as I was starting my new job, there was a change in

management, and while the new management was not very accessible, they were highly professional and a lot more focused on excelling in the hospitality business. I had been hired by those in the previous management group, but the new management saw potential in me and offered to sponsor my education at a very prestigious and highly regarded school, the Indian Institute of Management Bangalore (IIMB).

It was quite a sudden turn of events, but I felt a sense of lightness within. I was on the right path. I moved to Bangalore within a few days, still unable to believe that I was actually enrolled and would be recognized as an IIMB graduate. This was an amazing opportunity.

Located on a hundred-acre plot of land in the southern part of the city, IIMB, with its all-stone architecture, lush verdant woods, and landscaped gardens, was quite grand for an educational institute. Before entering the gates, I paused momentarily, taking in my surroundings. I noticed the *Gurkha*—a Nepali guard—standing at the gate, seemingly invisible to all the students who were passing in and out. Standing there, I felt like I was living another person's dream. I was so overwhelmed with a sense of gratitude that I greeted the *Gurkha* and shook his hand vigorously. He gaped at me as I entered the campus with a spring in my step and a song in my heart.

I was quite a carefree fellow in those days. I didn't dwell on my past mistakes; instead, I was focused on the future. I was my old self again. I joked around, made friends, and had fun with the other students, most of whom seemed to take life too seriously. I made some wonderful friends at IIMB, but most of the students were only driven to make the grade and that just wasn't my style.

Don't get me wrong, I did work hard and I took my studies seriously when it was required. But I also made time to relax and explore the city. I wanted to have balance, and as long as I was doing well in the program, I didn't see why I shouldn't. Other students didn't necessarily like my light-hearted approach. They felt I didn't deserve to be at IIMB, where thousands of students apply, but only a handful are accepted. I was not bookish like most of the students there, and those students were not exactly keen on seeing me succeed in my work. There is one particular example of this that still sticks out.

My roommates at IIMB had the habit of talking loudly during their study time. They would be going over all of the materials out loud, I would listen to them, and in that way, I learned all the material. Whatever they covered during the few hours of studying was enough for me to not only pass my exam but also pass with higher marks than they got! They weren't so happy about this, and at some point, they realized what I was doing. I suspect that they got together specifically to discuss how they could stop me. They decided to change their way of studying and no longer reviewed the material out loud.

When I realized what was happening, I figured out a solution. That has always been my strength. I instead made an agreement with another student to work with me a few hours before the test and tell me everything he learned. He would remember better by teaching me, and I would remember by listening to him. I passed.

My strength is my ability to think differently.

What happened to my roommates who had changed their way of studying, you ask? They failed. They changed their whole way of finding success just to try to thwart me, and it backfired spectacularly. After that, they went back to their old study habits and ignored me. So you see, my strength is in my way of thinking differently.

That story always makes me laugh, but it also highlights why I believe that finding a different way of doing things has led to my success. Rather than focusing on what others are doing, or worrying about how they behave, I choose to find my own solutions. I have always been more of a people-person, curious about the way the world functioned and how businesses thrived. Book knowledge is relevant, but what you learn out in the real world, when facing obstacles, is what makes a bigger difference in your life. Or at least that's what I've discovered in my journey.

"CULTURE" VERSUS "CULTURE"

There is one other moment that really stands out about my time at IIMB. A luxury hotel sponsored a competition. The judges included IIMB professors and senior hotel management. There was no prize beyond a certificate and recognition, but I have a highly competitive spirit—I had to win. I came up with a great premise for my project—something that was significantly based on my time at ITDC, the Veela, and at the Bengal Tiger.

My education and training in India gave me the impression that globally, hospitality functioned with a set of formulas which we were told to follow. When I was working in Singapore, I was told, "this is not India, we do things differently here." And when I returned to India, it was "this is not Singapore, we do things our way." I realized then that the formulas were not set in stone. Service processes are fluid, and there are no strict rules. It was ultimately the individual at the head of an establishment that decides what kind of hospitality their company will provide.

I proved that even though cultures are different across countries, if we can create a culturally efficient and neutral organization, we can co-exist and create a positive, comfortable environment for everyone. In any company, the culture will grow if there are people from different professions, educational backgrounds, cultures, and countries. This culture of diverse experiences enables you to expand your horizons and understand different perspectives. I worked damned hard on this project. It was important to me on a personal level as well, given my previous experiences with racism, cultural stereotyping, and other such issues.

Very few people understand the difference between culture and Culture. The former is just a general idea of how things work in one area or for one group, an idea in which a large number of outliers always seem to exist. Culture, with a capital C, is the idea that an environment can be built for *everyone*. I learned that if we used this model to develop an environment that was culturally appealing to a broad range of people, it would be long-lasting. That was the defining moment. I wanted to align with this concept of Culture and find ways to translate it into creating service policies that would create a venue where different nationalities from diverse backgrounds would find it comfortable to dine and leave having had a positive emotional experience.

I wanted to create a venue where different nationalities from diverse backgrounds would find it comfortable to dine and leave having had a positive emotional experience.

FEAR OF PEOPLE'S OPINIONS

As I worked on this concept, I would sit with my professor, revising and reworking the project multiple times until it was perfect. My fellow students were equally focused. They were hard-core competitors and every single student worked incredibly hard. There existed a strong competitive spirit, and many students made it clear that they would bring down others if it meant they could get ahead. Not a good environment to be honest. It didn't exactly foster a sense of teamwork or collaboration. In fact, it was in direct contrast to the type of environment I was trying to exemplify in my project.

Even with all the work I put in, all my revisions and attention to detail, it still came as a surprise that my project was selected. I was confident in my project's merits, but there were many other excellent projects, too. I think my winning the competition came as an even greater surprise to others than it did to me. I know I came across as a carefree guy, never the serious type, and suddenly my project was selected. They didn't understand the work I had put into it. There is no short cut to success, and when I put my mind to something, I put my whole heart and soul into it until I get it right. They didn't see my determination. They had judged me to be frivolous, when in actuality I was quite different. That's a main reason why being confident in yourself is so important. You can't let others' judgements stop you or let them instill doubt in yourself.

On the day of the ceremony, the judges announced why my project had been selected. They said it was practical and innovative. I received a standing ovation. It was such an amazing feeling of accomplishment. I bowed and thanked everyone. I was deeply grateful. With a deep, satisfied breath, as I walked down the stage, I noticed some sour expressions, filled with envy and resentment. I realized that in life, I would come across people who will be unhappy with me. In hindsight, I now recognize their jealousy fueled my determination to continue my climb in life.

So much of our lives revolve around creating impressions for people. We wonder what people say, their opinions and judgments. Fear of people's opinions (FOPO) has become big business in the teaching industry and as a self-help topic for books. How not to have FOPO seems to be difficult for many. My point is that it is not fear, but respect of people's opinions that is important. We need ROPO not FOPO.

FINAL THOUGHTS

There was still one thing that bothered me greatly. It kept me up at night. I was not sure whether to return to my employer, the Raj, who'd sponsored my IIMB education. I was returning to an employer where the politics that existed between the previous management and the new management were stifling. I wondered what it would be like to work for them. The previous luxury hotel management had had some objections toward me. They didn't think I was capable enough to handle the operations. They believed I wasn't up to the standards. What would the new management think? Sure, they had been impressed enough to send me to IIMB, but would it be enough? Would I have the freedom to share my ideas, or my vision? No doubt the hotel was a prestigious place to work and a secure company with a good position. But was it really for me?

Destiny takes us in directions we are meant to go. Mumbai was the city of dreams, and I felt that it was the best city to restart my journey. The following morning, I made the decision to return to the Raj Hotel. I had evolved from my mentorship and education at IIMB. I was armed with experience and proper training. Surely the luxury hotel management would find my input of great value, even if it took some time and work to get there.

Destiny takes us in directions we are meant to go.

I returned to Raj and started working diligently. For some time, I focused on my work and committed to creating an impact. My approach always lent itself to an innovative mindset, and I wanted to share my grand ideas. However, I felt restricted. When a work environment is unwilling to evolve or change, it becomes stagnant. I was blocked from expressing my views, unable to fully utilize my education and experience. I really struggled during that time. My job offered no scope for growth, and I couldn't explore my ideas like I had with the microbrewery. In those days, India had many restrictions: McDonald's had just opened, and Starbucks had not yet arrived. Worst of all, I was greatly bothered by the sense of guilt I constantly felt all the time because my heart was not in the job. *Had I become selfish?* I wondered. To be able to create with the freedom to innovate, I knew I had to be overseas.

My inner self was telling me it was time to make a move or I'd be stuck forever. My time at Raj also coincided with meeting and marrying my wife. When I met Anita in 1998 in Delhi, I had already worked overseas in Singapore and Bangkok. I was mature and I had experienced the extreme highs and lows that most people never have to face. Anita and I met at a friend's party and hit it off quickly. She admired my worldly knowledge and ability to hold a conversation. We had long chats about our life and expectations for the future. We connected on a deep level. When I was courting her in 1999, it was at a time when I was at the crossroads of my future. I was still wavering on my direction in hospitality and wasn't sure if I wanted to stay in Mumbai or move overseas.

In all the time that I traveled around the world prior to meeting Anita, one thing I needed the most in my life was stability. I realized more and more that *she* was my stabilizing factor. She was my quiet strength, and someone I could rely on in times when I needed clarity. My personal life was going wonderfully thanks to Anita, but my work life was not. And when I asked her to marry me, I realized that I had someone else to consider as I made my next career move. I wanted to work overseas again, and I wanted a position that better aligned with my ambition and skills. While I wavered, it was Anita who really decided our next move. On our honeymoon, she, too, fell in love with Bangkok and we decided it was where we wanted to start our life together. In order to make that happen as quickly as possible, I seized the first opportunity that allowed us to do that.

Chapter 7

A LATERAL STEP CAN LEAD TO THE NEXT STEP

In 2000, after Anita and I were married, we went to Phuket for our honeymoon. I was still rebuilding after the Singapore fiasco, so I had limited savings. I still wanted the best of everything in life for us. I couldn't be a lavish spender, but I wanted Anita to feel that she didn't lack for anything. While we were in Phuket she said, "Everyone tells me the best shopping is in Bangkok. Why don't we go there?" I couldn't say no to my new wife.

We took a special trip to Bangkok and enjoyed our time there. While we shopped and interacted with the beautiful people of Thailand, Anita fell in love with the city, just as had I previously. She wanted to make it her home. So as we shopped and bargained in the street markets, we shared our desire to move to the city with the warm and friendly locals. A kindly shopkeeper suggested that we visit the Erawan Shrine, make a wish, and pay respects to Lord Brahma. It is believed that whoever goes there and makes a wish will have it fulfilled. We did go to the Erawan Shrine and prayed. Then we returned to India.

A few months later, the Divine granted our wish and we moved to Bangkok.

My first step was to join the Royalty Park (name has been changed) serviced apartments business. Like the Raj Group, Royalty Park offered a secure position with several perks, but still lacked some of the space for innovation I would have preferred. I also knew the benefits were what Anita and I needed at that time, and I always have believed that lateral steps can lead to the next opportunity. So even though there wasn't much incentive for growth or development, I was very happy to take the job.

When I say there were perks, I really mean it. At that point, I was still recovering financially after losing everything. This position allowed us to move to Bangkok quickly, which was our primary goal. However, it also provided a salary that allowed me to pay off my credit card bills. It was such a weight off my shoulders. The company also provided us with a car. It wasn't anything fancy, but Anita loved that car.

We had a lot of good times while I worked there. We lived within walking distance of my office. I would pick up vegetables from the vegetable seller right outside the building, walk home, and Anita would cook up something wonderful every night. It was a simpler time, but we really enjoyed it. It was what we needed, right when we needed it.

Even though things were going very well, I never forgot my ultimate goals. I wanted more in life. I wanted to give Anita everything she could ever desire. So while I worked very hard for Royalty Park Apartments, I was always on the lookout for the right opportunity. I wouldn't settle for just anything. Sometimes, having the perfect secure position gives you the freedom to look for and *wait for* the perfect opportunity. Given my mistakes, I had learned how important that is. I wasn't going to make that mistake again.

THE LATERAL LEADS TO THE NEXT

One day, in April 2003, the Asia-Pacific President of an American Restaurant Group and their head of development approached me with an offer to be the general manager of the Regent Hotel in Bangkok. I enthusiastically agreed. This was what I had been waiting for. It was a great opportunity. Once I received confirmation of the job offer, I resigned from the Royalty Park company.

I was already settled in Bangkok, and my beautiful wife provided the stability and support that enabled me to climb the next rung in my career ladder. The Regent Hotel was supposed to be in the State Tower, a skyscraper in the heart of Bangkok city. I was looking forward to my new position. Unfortunately, the deal fell through. I was told that the Regent Hotel was no longer in the picture. Instead, the Hotel Suites (name has been changed) would be in the State Tower, and they already had a team in place. There was no room for me there.

American Restaurant Group's team offered me two other job options, but they were in other countries. My wife and I were already settled in Bangkok and we didn't want to move away from Thailand. They then introduced me to the Bualert family. They were the mother-daughter team who were originally going to hire me to be the general manager of the Regent Hotel if they had acquired the space. They were a well-known family and had numerous businesses and investments. Since that deal didn't work out, they showed me a project on the rooftop of the State Tower, called the Dome. They were interested in creating restaurants there and asked if I would consider that project instead. I wasn't sure, so I didn't commit. I knew very little about the background of this skyscraper and I wanted to research it a bit more. I needed to be sure I could create the right concept and have the right freedom to do the project justice.

The State Tower was built in 1997. It was a grand structure of over three million square feet. The sixty-eight floors with a golden dome on the rooftop gave the building its character and charm. But it had sat vacant for six years. It was essentially just a shell, and we would be starting from scratch. To put this Dome project in perspective, no one thought this could work for several reasons. First, both the Regent Hotel and Hotel Suites groups had previously declined to build anything there. Second, many top chefs had told the owners that no restaurant was going to do well on such a high floor.

This information would put off most people from taking on the project, but the fact that the Dome was such a challenge and had received negative comments was precisely the reason I began to feel a sense of excitement about taking it on. Within the realms of the impossible, I could make something possible. But I still needed more time to reflect on those possibilities. It was therefore perfect timing that my wife and I had planned a short relaxing getaway to Bali. There's no place like a holiday to bring creative ideas to the surface of the mind.

Within the realms of the impossible,
I could make something possible.

In Bali, we stayed at a villa at the Ritz Carlton and had the most relaxing time. It wasn't just the ambience, but also the excellent restaurants and high-quality service. There was one restaurant in particular that was very thought-provoking. To get there, we had to walk down a hundred steps to reach the dining area. It was an unusual concept. From what I had always seen, the norm was that one should climb up, not down toward the restaurant. Though the restaurant was very casual, I was able to see and understand its model was to combine excellent service with an emotional experience.

Though it was quite late in the evening by the time we finished dinner, I called the Dome project owners and agreed to take on the assignment. Even now, I can still feel the excitement I had eighteen years ago. I was so excited to create a hospitality environment that went way beyond food. I knew the emotional experience would matter more. In Bangkok, there is no doubt that the service and attentiveness are above average, but at the end of the day, the restaurants were just focused on the food and beverage aspect. I wanted to offer more than that.

In May 2003, I was ready to write a new chapter of my life. I signed on the dotted line, committing to the project. I received US$3 million in seed money, shook hands with the Bualerts, and thanked them for placing their trust in me. They were taking a huge chance on me. They had given me near complete freedom. Finally, I had to the opportunity to really marry creativity and innovation in new and exciting ways, all to accomplish the "impossible."

Despite the many negatives about the Dome, I was prepared to do what it took to make it successful. I understood that this project would make or break me. My gut was telling me that if I got it right, this project would define my position in the industry. It felt like this would be another turning point in my life. If I could pull it off, the Dome would pave my way to the heights of success. But first, I had to face the challenges, and there were many.

First, the Bualerts wanted me to open a restaurant that December, which was just seven months away. I agreed! (What else could I do?) During those early weeks, I received lots of advice—some suggested to add a canopy over the open-air space. However, I wanted to enhance the natural beauty, not cover it up. I already had the idea, theme, and vision, so I didn't need to waste time on a concept or design. I knew that if I got the right people, everything would come together smoothly.

My vision built upon many moments of inspiration from my past. For example, I recalled meeting a water designer many years previously. They designed water features that brought out the aesthetic beauty of water in a natural way. I asked the team how they were able to become so successful and popular. "It is simple," they said, "water is meant to flow. We see where and how it wants to flow within a space, and we create the environment around that."

At the Dome, the soft breeze needed to flow freely, not be blocked. The fabulous view was meant to be admired, not covered up. The natural beauty was what made this rooftop unique. So just like those water feature designers, my goal was to create a destination dining space that was a sensory celebration that flowed with the breeze instead of fighting it.

I decided that the first restaurant at the Dome had to be an open-air model. Besides the outdoor dining space, the view from the other dining areas was going to be extraordinary, and yet have unique perspectives from each seat. This idea led to the birth of the Sky Bar, which was slightly elevated, higher than the restaurant, but still overlooking the city. With the vision of the restaurant and bar vivid in my mind, I got started.

The 15th of May, 2003 is etched in my mind. That particular day, I stepped into the State Tower lobby, took the lift up to the top floor, 810 feet above the city, and stared at the huge, abandoned space. There was a stray dog and a cat lurking about. The site was completely dilapidated with dripping, rusty pipes, gray, peeling walls, and dark patches on the ceiling—it was a disaster zone.

In that dark, dank ruin, I envisioned a stunning restaurant overlooking a breathtaking view of the city. I stood there. Still and silent. I closed my eyes and felt the wind on my face. A name came to mind—Sirocco—a Mediterranean breeze. It was the perfect choice. I imagined the space filled with diners enjoying themselves. The tinkle of dripping pipes transformed into the clinking of champagne glasses. The lighting would sparkle through the glass windows, not through cracks in the walls. Music would make the ambience heavenly. The restaurant was going to be a unique magical experience. There would be an aura of fun and laughter as guests enjoyed the indoor and outdoor areas.

In my mind's eye, I saw class, grace, and beauty in every gray wall. I saw diners treated with the best service, quality cuisine, and the best wines. It was all there, vivid, like a film reel in my mind. The whole design concept was clear in my head. All I had to do was translate it into reality.

At the same time, every challenge that I would face came to the forefront of my thoughts. Many had said this was not worth the effort. This was going to be the greatest test of my life. I realized that in order to deliver on my promise to open in six months, I had to strategize. I had to run projects simultaneously.

It takes a certain caliber and level of self-discipline to handle different tasks simultaneously. Part of my process was to work backward. I had my final goal and I had my starting budget and resources. I just had to fill in the gaps between the two. I worked backward, step by step. If that was my goal, what steps were required to get there? I planned it all out. Most people work forward from their starting point and that's why they fail—because they don't know the next step, or they get sidetracked by side projects. I now had a series of steps I needed to complete. To that end, I decided I would work eighteen hours a day. I created nine compartments of tasks for the Dome project. Each day, I allocated two hours per task. However, as with any project, there are unforeseen complications.

One particularly time-consuming detail that I had not considered was that all correspondence was in Thai. Whenever I received a memo or any communication, I could not read them. (Google translate was not yet a thing!) I had to hire a secretary to translate all of the paperwork and documents for me. After returning home, despite eighteen long, grueling hours at work, I would read the translations. Each day, I was completely immersed in taking a disciplined approach to work. I was working seven days a week and not sleeping more than five hours a day. At times it was tedious to multi-task and handle communications, but it had to be done.

I was facing challenges from every direction. Whenever the word "challenge" comes up, the solution is already there waiting to be discovered within the challenge itself. My mentor's words came back to me during this stage. Santiani would say, "when facing a big task, break it into small parts and with each task, a solution will be easier to find." I focused on dealing with issues task by task.

Adequate preparation and research were needed before any task could begin. I flew to London to get a few more concepts and ideas that covered some of the details. I also would meet with the interior design team; we had to ensure there would be a smooth workflow. We covered issues with the kitchen, ambience, service processes, and other related problems. Finer details were also discussed at length. The whole project from planning to implementation had been broken down into segments.

The Dome's space was large enough to accommodate over one thousand guests every day. Even though I was laughed at for expecting those kinds of numbers, I still continued to plan for it. I never doubted that we would someday have that many guests.

In the midst of all the work, there were critical comments, discouraging remarks, and an attitude that I was wasting time and money. Through their contacts at the Hotel Suites, the owners provided me with a team. However, the fifteen-member-team didn't believe in my ability to deliver within the specified timeline. When they asked about the schedule, and I responded, "December." They then asked, "Which year?" They laughed at me when I told them it was this year. It was impossible, they said. Like buzzing bees, the words would revolve around my head ... "How can you do this?" ... "You will not be able to finish this job." ... "Why are you doing it like this?" ... it went on and on. I could have defended myself, reasoned and explained everything I was doing. But I had no time to waste. I had already discovered that the fear of other people's opinions would only hold me back. My ability to stay single-mindedly focused was all that mattered to me, so I didn't waste my time trying to explain it to the nonbelievers. They wouldn't get it anyway.

One important lesson I'd learned from Santiani was that if you have a team that doesn't believe in you, you will not succeed. If people do believe in you, half the battle is already won. I began to organize my own team. One that would understand and support my vision. One that would do what it takes to get the job done.

In all that bustle and buzz, the one thing that stood out was my conviction. A strong, focused conviction that this grand vision of mine could be achieved. Even the owners were convinced that I would be able to make it happen. Often, I would go back to them with updates and new requirements for Sirocco. They would offer their contacts and connections to support my ongoing efforts. They were incredibly supportive, and I was and am very grateful for that. Despite the negativity, setbacks, and other concerns, for those six months until the restaurant was to be opened, I just went off the radar. I focused only on my immediate tasks. My wife was a saint for supporting me during that time. It couldn't have been easy on her.

When I look back at my experiences, struggling for four years, both in India and Singapore, being mentored by Joe Santiani in the US, and then my transformation with the Dome, I can't help but notice the impact that of all those lessons I'd learned in the past, along with intense personal focus, came into play here. They are the keys to achieving with conviction and courage. I never lost sight of my goal.

GETTING THE JOB DONE

To accomplish the construction phase of the project, I managed to engage a well-known London-based construction company who agreed to handle every aspect. We signed the design and construction contract and I thought that was that. Almost a month later, they sent a letter of regret. They would not be able to complete the project that year. It was a setback, and no doubt, I was shaken up. Should I admit defeat? Spoiler-alert, I did not.

Instead, I racked my brain for any contacts that I could call upon. I recalled I had met someone in Singapore, a few years ago. It was one of those chance meetings when one strikes up a conversation with a stranger at a bar and never really expects to meet again. We had a nice friendly chat. At that time, he was a director working in a construction company. He had given me his business card, not really thinking it would be of any use. Luckily, I had kept it.

In my current desperate situation, he was my last resort. I had to take a chance and call him. I didn't even know if he would remember me. Still, I had to try. I scanned through my collection of business cards and found his. I called him up and learned that he had moved to London, as chairman of the parent company that owned the construction company I'd originally hired. After connecting with him, he remembered me right away, and that I had bought him a beer. Wonder of wonders, he agreed to fast track the project!

Who would have thought that the one person who I hadn't in my wildest dreams expected to cross paths with again would be the one man to lift my project off the ground? Literally! There's a lesson to be learned here: sometimes we make friends with strangers, it might be a chance encounter, but whichever way we look at it, as one of life's mysteries or that everything happens for a reason, we must keep our contacts. Who knows, someday that stranger could make a huge impact on your life.

The greatest power, even in today's world, comes from the human mind.

That chairman was so committed he mobilized a team right away. He flew in four experts from Australia and Singapore. Within thirty-six hours, those experts were in Bangkok assessing the situation. They prepared a logistics timeline that involved both construction and restaurant interiors.

"How can four people make this project work?" I was asked. Little did those critics realize that the greatest power, even in today's world, comes from the human mind. If the right four people decided to take on this project, and work hard, they could be unstoppable.

Besides the various materials, like concrete, a hundred tons of steel had to be lifted to the top and then bolted to reinforce the foundations. Transporting the steel and other materials, removing debris, and using a single crane lift was an onerous task. Work was in twenty-four-hour shifts. The night shift was transporting materials back and forth, while the actual construction and design work was carried out during the day shifts. Sirocco was unfolding at a pace that was in tune with my thudding heart. Would it be completed in time?

While the exteriors and design were being created, I hired a New York-based kitchen consultant who was an expert in the food service industry. The location of the restaurant on the top floor of a high rise had certain restrictions. No gas stoves or any gas-related gadgets were allowed at that height. Every kitchen appliance had to be electrical and be ordered from overseas. My consultant handled every part of the kitchen. It was expensive but worth every dollar.

This was another one of the finer lessons I learned from Santiani—when you hire consultants and experts, don't skimp on fees. At the end of the day, if you pay for quality, you save in the long run. That consultant proved to be a valuable resource, and still is to this day. Quality over quantity wins every time.

For the interiors of the restaurants, I reached out to many interior designers, but they needed a longer timeline. Others had their own design concepts which we rejected. Finally, we found an office designer who was aligned with what we were conceptualizing and who agreed to create Sirocco the way *we* wanted it.

There was no time to construct first and design later. With every segment of my castle up in the air, everything was going to be done simultaneously, including the interiors.

Meanwhile, a friend of the owners, a designer of the Hotel Suites, criticized my ability (or rather, the lack of it) and claimed I was taking them for a ride. The Bualerts listened but didn't act on her remarks. The designer even went as far as to say that I was a *farang*—a non-White person, an Indian, and therefore someone who would amount to nothing of value. It was a very discriminatory remark. The bottom line was that the owners were advised to reconsider their faith in me and my project. They remained quiet to the external criticism and kept their trust in me.

The owners provided a few suggestions for the Dome based on advice they received from well-wishers: plastic folding chairs, a few tables, papaya salad, and satays (a popular southeast Asian dish). It was also suggested to them that they charge a ticket for the view. It was a safe bet, but it didn't fit in my vision. The State Tower wasn't exactly the ideal place for customers to take an elevator to the top floor to eat a meal, especially not one that was available on every street corner. There was another suggestion, that we open a nightclub in the space, but again that was not what I had planned. Criticism about what I was doing, and how crazy it was, was a constant part of the day. Still, the Bualerts trusted my plan and let me have my way.

My goal was to make the world sit up and take notice.

After a few months, the Bualerts opened a café in the lobby of the building that had a few wooden chairs and tables. The president of the Hotel Suites came to meet me. He presented a bouquet of flowers and said: "Wow, now I know where you are spending all that money!" His remark was sarcastic, but I smiled broadly, took the flowers, and gracefully ignored him.

This kind of negativity struck a chord within me, but it was more of a spark to move forward and prove to every naysayer that I had it in me to do what I promised I would do.

Sirocco was all about dignity and respect.

Any competent business requires respect for every individual in the organization, valuing their skills without judging their color or creed; building Sirocco was also building my strength and my ability to face these kinds of discriminatory and unethical behaviors. My goal was to make the world sit up and take notice. I especially wanted the bigots of the world to see that an Indian had the capability to open a non-Indian restaurant. That an Indian can create quality fine dining menus and cater to the needs of all classes of society. Sirocco was all about dignity and respect.

STIFF COMPETITION

In a city which was already inundated with restaurants, and a market known for cheap venues, I was facing competition before I had even begun. Also, to make matters worse, Bangkok was in the midst of recovering from the SARS virus in July 2003. According to the Tourism and Sports Minister of Thailand, the country is estimated to have lost forty billion baht in tourism revenues during the first half of 2003. Tourist arrivals had declined by 1.6 million or 30 percent compared to the same period the previous year. All I could think was, *That doesn't mean that the tourists will never come back.* The Dome was going to provide an amazing sensory experience that would be totally different and would attract tourists back to Thailand.

A very important part of the restaurant business is to figure out what customer expectations are and how to meet or exceed them. I invited a focus group of customers from Singapore, Hong Kong, and Thailand to visit the site. This would provide a greater understanding of customer behavior and what they expected.

We had invited these focus groups to share their opinion. Everyone said the restaurant had no view. Many people would have listened to the focus groups and changed the concept. Even the Gallup Poll report recommended that we should reconsider doing the restaurant. The poll came to this conclusion after listening to five focus groups—one each from Hong Kong and Singapore, and three from Thailand. Everyone said this restaurant had no view. I listened to the conclusions, but it only gave me ideas on what needed to be improved. It didn't stop me from pursuing the dream.

I had no intention of ignoring the focus groups of the Gallup Report; the point is that I am not easily dissuaded from achieving my goals. I respect and appreciate public opinion, but I am not afraid of it. All it does is help me see problems I may have overlooked and find solutions. In this particular instance, we used one hundred tons of steel to elevate the floor and it created a remarkable difference in the ambience. Later on, Wallpaper Magazine would say that Sirocco had the most spectacular view they'd ever seen.

---

*I respect and appreciate public opinion,
but I am not afraid of it.*

I also hired a marketing company and gave the marketing director a tour of the site. The director wasn't exactly on the same page with my concept and business model. She scoffed at my pricing plan. In fact, to prove her point, she invited me and my team to a popular local restaurant that served chili crabs. I knew about this place; they were famous for this delicacy. The marketing director made her point, that the total bill was less than what I was going to price just the crab dish at Sirocco. I simply said, "They are selling food. We are selling the experience."

My conviction about my own ideas and abilities transformed me. I was no longer a follower but was instead in tune with the pulse of the moment, as a leader. A leader is capable of envisioning a new dimension and a new perspective. It wasn't easy to convince and educate those who felt they knew better. I was constantly expected to prove myself.

THE FINAL RESULT

The Dome became the destination I had envisioned. It was a sensory celebration that was visual, kinesthetic, olfactory, and gustatory. There was just one missing element—auditory. To complete the entire emotional experience at the top of the skyscraper, I needed music to add to the ambience. With no ceiling and no walls, we created a platform stage for a live band. It was the icing on the cake. The whole space had a magical feel.

On November 30th, the Sirocco rooftop restaurant and the Sky Bar officially opened with a grand celebration featuring a show of fireworks. It was a state-of-the-art restaurant, and a fabulous team had put all of it together. Sirocco was a fine dining establishment, ornamented by breathtaking views of the sky and the city. It was lavish; the whole industry of hoteliers suddenly noticed this new kid on the block. All the guests were impressed and were mesmerized with the layout, the décor, and, of course, the view. In fact, every segment of the space was aesthetically designed and put to optimum use. Everyone was congratulating the owners and me for the unique design and concept.

Sirocco was recognized, at that time, as the fourth rooftop restaurant in the world. It was the first of many innovative ideas that became my signature. I was soon labeled as a maverick and a visionary in hospitality. People who once chose to ignore me and my novel ideas, wanted to get to know me. It was vindicating to achieve that level of recognition.

The owners were impressed and happy that everything worked out on schedule, without me asking for a penny more than the seed money. When I asked the senior owner why she had so much faith in me despite all of the criticism, she simply said: "High risk, high gain." I was their best bet. I smiled.

The sky is not the limit; it is limitless.

Yes, it was a glorious moment to see that I had achieved what I had set out to do. I was on top of the world. I believe that if you have the right mindset and resiliency, there's nothing and no one to stop you from climbing higher. And you know what, the sky is not the limit; it is limitless.

INNOVATIVELY RESILIENT

After the party was over, Sirocco was a popular topic. What I achieved with Sirocco had never been done before in Asia. I had created a trendsetter in rooftop dining, and I was aiming to be the best globally. I should have been feeling ecstatic and proud of the compliments. While I kept up the smile and the happy demeanor, I still felt that a vital element was missing. In terms of financial returns, Sirocco did well. The owners expected fifteen thousand baht in revenues each day, and we achieved seven times that! Still, I wasn't happy, and I did not join in the celebrations.

The chef came to me and said, "Deepak, why are you putting so much pressure on us? You've exceeded everyone's expectations. Everyone is happy except you." Sirocco was fabulous in every sense of the word, but I felt there was something missing.

The owners, too, were asking me, "Deepak what's your problem? No one has achieved revenue numbers like you have. The whole team is celebrating."

I wasn't happy because I had envisioned a concept, a specific idea, that wasn't coming through. I was also thinking long term. What I had created would not last. It was not sustainable. Sirocco was a novel idea, and anyone would be interested to check out the new restaurant with the spectacular view. It was great that we had such a fabulous response, but in my eyes, this was not a consistent model. No matter how great we were, I was concerned that if there was competition, we would face a dip. And eventually, we would lose market share.

What was missing in Sirocco was the soul. No doubt, the restaurant design was built as I had envisioned, but it is service that creates the emotional experience, and that was not coming through. To do that, one needs a cold calculated approach to create an emotional experience. But first, let's backtrack a little to understand my philosophy.

TRANSLATE CULTURE INTO SERVICE

I've talked about culture before, but as with anything, as my career progressed, I've also expanded on that original concept.

I had to adjust it to account for the advent of social media and technology. The world is more connected than ever before. We have a wider access to different cultures and people because of technology. With social media, we are able to discover so much more in terms of products, services, and knowledge. The future is based on respecting cultures and creating an impact to suit specific customer tastes. So how do we embrace culture? Translating culture into a service means *inclusiveness*. Today the world is talking a lot about Environmental, Social, and (Corporate) Governance (ESG), and Diversity, Equity, and Inclusion (DE&I), but all of these things boil down to inclusiveness.

My education and training in India gave me the impression that globally, hospitality functioned with a set of formulas that I was no longer satisfied with. When I was working in Singapore, I was told, "This is not India, we do things differently here." I realized then that the formulas were not set in stone. Service processes were fluid, and it was up to me, as the head of an establishment, to decide what kind of hospitality we were going to provide.

There are certain kinds of people who see the world as solid. I see it as fluid. Many people feel the world is rigid and inflexible. When they face failures, they tend to give up. They also accept that this is the way life is supposed to be and choose not to persist further. The way I think is different. When I face rejection or a disadvantage, I see possibilities to explore beyond. Methods can be created to turn rejection into a positive response and disadvantage to an advantage. Over the years in hospitality, I have faced "it cannot be done" as an answer many times. I always found ways to make it happen anyway.

When I returned to India and started working there again, I experienced that same response, "This is not America or

Singapore. We do things differently here." This cultural attitude did not deflate my ambitions, in fact it gave me the opportunity to see the hospitality industry differently, to explore my horizons of possibilities. I could transform, innovate, and make changes in unique ways. But first I had to create a new perception. This would be no easy task.

Sirocco, let me be clear, is a fine dining restaurant. Customers intentionally go to a fine dining establishment because they are willing to pay for more than just the food. They are seeking a high-quality experience. Fine dining means that the servers have to be exceptional. The staff has to appear experienced and knowledgeable, which extends beyond the menu and to the restaurant business itself.

When I had decided on the fine dining concept, it was because I saw a gap in the service attitude. It took time to develop and change our servers' psyches to the attitude that every guest is to be treated with the same respect and attention. There was to be no bias. I was proactively changing a norm that had been conditioned in everyone's minds for a long time. In Bangkok, customers were defined and treated by status, whether they were CEOs, celebrities, or the who's who of society. They were fawned over when they entered any dining establishment or hotel. There was a culture of bias toward certain types of clienteles, some were bowed to while others ignored. I was disrupting this unbalanced style of hospitality.

At either end of the spectrum, I was sending an unspoken message. It was right to insist on equality. Not just servers, waiters, and restaurant staff should be treated with respect, but also every client, VIP or not, who stepped into the restaurant should be treated with respect and given that same level of attention. The right of equality means respect to everyone.

HIRING THE RIGHT PEOPLE

When guests dined at Sirocco, I didn't want them to just say, "This is great food or a great restaurant," I wanted everyone to say, "This was a fabulous experience!" However, we were receiving negative comments instead of compliments. I was reading guest reviews and noticed a few comments that were unusual. One of them was that the Thai fried rice was not good. How could that be? Sirocco is a Mediterranean restaurant. Where did the Thai fried rice come from?!

Feeling frustrated, but maintaining a calm demeanor, I spoke with the chef. He said he never served any fried rice. We perused the menu and realized that there was one dish which was fish on a bed of paella. The diner mistook the paella for fried rice. It was a wake-up call for me that I had to be proactive in creating a very specific kind of brand awareness. I was building on the fact that I was not selling a plate of food but a luxurious experience. Sirocco represented a combination of these things. The right perception had to be created, and that needed to start with the serving staff.

To create a lasting impression, we must listen to the customers, and to have soul, we have to train our employees. That was when I started to add some science into creating a soulful experience. The staff had to be seamless in back-end operations. In the visible part of the restaurant, the customers would experience something unique and emotional.

When we were still in the planning stages, instead of looking for famous top chefs, I was looking for someone who wanted to *become* a top chef. The search became easier—not just for chefs but for the rest of the kitchen staff we hired. Hiring was not based solely on their résumé but became more about their

personal drive to achieve. I wanted to hire people who were motivated and had the resiliency to succeed. I was looking for a
very specific type of person. I finally hired a sous-chef. His salary
was higher than mine. I didn't mind; he had skill and talent. I
was glad he was equally enthusiastic to be a part of my team. He
believed in Sirocco. Unfortunately, I did not follow this philosophy when I was hiring the servers.

Part of the problem at that stage was that the project was
huge, and word was spreading that an Indian was the head of
the project. In Thailand, these kinds of cutting-edge projects
were usually handled by a European or an American. It *shouldn't*
have mattered, but my nationality became a talking point. Once
again, I was facing obstacles based solely on my race. Convinc-
ing people to come and work for the Dome project, where the
owners are Thai and the head of the project is Indian, proved
to be difficult. I had to find high quality employees and staff
willing to take a chance. I was successful with the kitchen staff,
but not with the initial group of serving staff.

In that first week of Sirocco's opening, the service was average. I knew I was trying to fit a square peg in a round hole. It
wasn't easy for the staff members to align with my concept of
equal treatment for all guests. More time was needed to train
them, but Sirocco was already up and running, and I wanted
the servers to learn quickly. It wasn't happening to my level of
expectation. I needed to apply the same philosophy I'd used to
hire our chefs to the process of hiring our servers.

The following day I called a staff meeting. Eleven of them
looked at me with a blank expression when I conveyed my
points. They were unable to grasp the level of service I was expecting of them. One of the staff members said, "Either you
stop telling us what to do, or we resign." It was 3:00 p.m. Sirocco was supposed to open in three hours. I wouldn't be able

to handle it without support, and they knew that. I was silent. I saw that the rest of the staff had the same "don't tell me what to do" expression. I responded calmly, "Please leave." I turned and walked away.

That's when I returned to my desk, sat there and said to myself, "This whole operation cannot run like this, it needs the right people and has to run like a well-oiled machine." I needed to apply the same philosophy I'd used to hire our chefs to the process of hiring our servers.

I realized that to build a restaurant is one thing, but to maintain the standards is another. It requires strategy, vision, and, most of all, the right people. A bit overwhelmed but still focused on the restaurant opening in less than three hours, I called up a trusted and intelligent staff member I knew from a few years ago. She had worked for me as a manager when I was running Bräuhaus. She was a smart woman and had managed the business well. I asked her if she would like to work for me. She said yes right away, but she couldn't start immediately. In her current job, she was required to give a three-month notice.

I offered to cover the costs associated. "Resign now, I will compensate you. I will pay for the notice period. Be here in one hour. Get on your motorcycle and come. Come with ten staff." She arrived with ten staff members, and we opened the restaurant at 6:00 p.m., right on schedule. She has been with me throughout her tenure, for almost two decades, and only recently retired at age sixty.

In this industry, people are the most important asset for building a brand. Making the decision to hire her, even though under dire circumstances, was one of the best decisions I have made in my life. I then hired senior management and Sirocco's staff grew from fourteen to sixty. Again, I employed that same philosophy of hiring based on attitude rather than just their résumé. With an efficient system in place, running smoothly, I was able to look at the big picture and focus on other aspects of the business.

BUILDING AN EMOTIONAL EXPERIENCE

Our goal was that if we wanted to give the best emotional experience to our guests, we had to be objective and take into consideration all kinds of feedback. We decided that our marketing would be done by all our customers and our employees. We interlinked the customer experience with our training needs for our employees. We got customers to fill out a survey online. In this way we were able to pinpoint the weaknesses and understand the training needs. We could not take an anecdotal approach to dealing with three hundred customers every day, so we created a very consistent method of measuring the quality of service. And we took every single online customer feedback seriously.

I usually prefer not to take anecdotal feedback from customers, but as with most things, there is always an exception. In January, 2004, a group of executives and corporate professionals came to dine at Sirocco. They were dining al fresco and having a great time ordering champagne, caviar, and other entrées. It suddenly started raining, which was quite unusual for that time of the year. The executives were drenched and left in a hurry. The bill was close to US$4,000, and they hadn't paid.

The following day, the same group of businessmen returned, but this time they were in shorts and t-shirts, and brought their umbrellas. They offered to pay for the dinner from the day before. I hesitated. I told them I wouldn't charge them as their meal was interrupted by the rain. The chairman of the worldwide company insisted that they would dine that day only if I agreed to charge them for the previous day's bill as well. He also told me he would give me some valuable advice. I accepted.

His feedback was first, to arrange parasols for the outdoor dining tables, and second, to offer the customer a complementary meal and a rain check voucher for a glass of champagne on their next visit if the weather is a problem. He said, "ninety-five percent of diners will pay." I took his advice seriously; we implemented his suggestions. The chairman was right, the diners paid most of the time.

This brings up an interesting point about listening that I've held on to all these years. When we listen, we learn. Listening is an art; it is not just about hearing, but actively understanding, being present, and connecting with the individual who is sharing his or her knowledge. This particular executive gave me an idea. If I had not listened to him, I think Sirocco would not be what it is today, and I would not be writing this book. The point is that what he shared, and I applied, created an immediate emotional connection with the customer. The irony is that the executive had no knowledge of the hospitality industry, yet he gave me excellent advice as a well-wisher. I could have easily ignored him, but I did not. We often listen to people who call themselves experts, but we also need to be mindful of the non-experts. They can share valuable advice, too.

When we listen, we learn. Listening is an art; it is not just about hearing, but actively understanding, being present, and connecting with the individual who is sharing his or her knowledge.

This situation with these businessmen also inspired me to take marketing in a different direction. We began to advertise not just in the hospitality trade publications, but also in business magazines. We were the first hospitality company in Thailand that started promoting in the business sector. We also advertised on TV channels targeting a different brand of clientele. All because I *listened.*

CORRELATIONS CREATE IMPACT

In management, the biggest tool I have learned is correlation. It is the ability to see an opportunity and then correlate it with work. This applies to how you talk to people and correlate with what needs to be changed—just like the executive did when he gave me advice on the parasols and the rain-check vouchers.

I realized that to stay ahead and for consistency of creating an impact with our brand, we couldn't continue with the same marketing company. They didn't get what we were trying to do and were damaging the perception of Sirocco rather than helping. How? I wanted to do something that never had been done before. I'd seen an opportunity, and I became confident that I could take our marketing to the next level. I had already devised a plan, a plan that a restaurant had never done before. I went to my boss and asked her for a million baht to do a full-page advertisement. It was a large sum of money at that time, equivalent to approximately thirty thousand US dollars.

"Are you crazy?" she asked.

Without conviction, you cannot achieve bigger things.

What I had in mind was indeed risky, but to create an impact, this was the ideal solution. I had great conviction that a change in perception was what was needed. Santiani's words came to mind often in those days: "Without conviction you cannot achieve bigger things."

The owner looked at me skeptically when she handed me the check for one million baht.

What was my full-page advertisement? "Even after dark the sky changes color."

"EVEN AFTER DARK THE SKY CHANGES COLOR"

This became the tagline for our restaurant. We'd launched it in a full-page advertisement in the Bangkok Post. It was impressive. If you think about this tagline in real life situations, anyone's journey is bumpy with failures, and there will be obstacles that will get you down. The length of the failures will vary. But even during failure, change is happening. The sky will change color, every minute, every second—there is a change happening. We just need to be aware of the opportunities. Be aware of the weaknesses and be conscious of becoming fluid and adapt. That's when success will come faster than we realize.

The advertisement looked like a simple message to readers but there was a deeper meaning behind it. First of all, a full-page advertisement in the local newspaper was unheard of in those days in Bangkok. In fact, construction businesses and other big executives of the city would only advertise with a half or quarter page. The full-page advertisement caused a buzz. Secondly, the words resonated with the people who would enjoy the exclusive and unique quality of the dining experience it evoked; this one sentence aroused interest from a breed of guests who understood my concept.

Sirocco became a globally recognized restaurant. We were on the cover of Wallpaper Magazine, not just the Thailand edition, but worldwide. All this popularity was the result of that one full-page advertisement and the cover story resulting from it. In addition, there was word-of-mouth publicity. Everyone in our organization was celebrating. Again, it got me thinking . . . how long would all of this buzz work? I had to add more value to the dining concept.

I faced many negative comments when we opened the restaurant, comments such as the service was not up to standards, or the quality of food wasn't up to expectations. I took every single comment into consideration and created a correlation as to how to improve on all those aspects. I decided to hire a customer research company to get to the root of what really was bothering our customers. We discovered that the issue was not the food or service, it was the pricing. Customers were hesitant to tell us that we were overpriced. I didn't change anything on the menu, including the prices. Instead, I worked out a plan to create an environment that encouraged like-minded people who would appreciate our dining experience.

First, we implemented a dress code policy. At that time in Thailand, no restaurant had a dress code policy. On the surface of it, the policy seemed like a bad idea: clientele would drop, and people would not want to dine at Sirocco. But the opposite happened. When I lecture at business schools, and share my dress code policy, no one yet has been able to answer why this policy is so effective. So let me explain: When we started the dress code policy, it was like a sifter. It filtered out those who were not in tune with what Sirocco had to offer. From that moment on, there were fewer complaints about the food. What we received instead were compliments and appreciation. Both the pricing and dress code policies became a unique way of positioning Sirocco, bringing in the right profile of customers.

FINAL THOUGHTS

The dynamic effect of the advertisement in the local paper, *Even after dark the sky changes color,* added value to how we were perceived. This was the turning point for Sirocco and what would eventually become the *lebua* brand. We had achieved a lot of "firsts" with Sirocco—first to advertise with a full-page ad, first champagne bar, and so on. That tagline created history for the company, and for me personally in both my career and life. Even after dark, the sky *did* change color. My life was now full of color, full of brightness, full of enthusiasm.

I was finally happy that Sirocco was on the right track. We had created a product that was more than just a restaurant. One would think that the only pain I faced was in planning and opening the restaurant. In reality, it would be another challenge to ensure the high level of sustainability, consistency of service, and efficiency that I expected of the company each and every day. Yet facing challenges and innovating in the face of them was my forte. I thrived on the challenge, and I was ready to face the next one.

Chapter 8

THE MILLION BAHT DINNER

It was an exhilarating time in 2007. Since 2004, I had become a star of the Bangkok Post and was featured in lifestyle magazines and other media.

Sirocco at the State Tower became a phenomenon. Competitors were bristling with envy that Deepak Ohri, a recent entry into the business, a man who doesn't belong with the elite class, had come in and shaken up the system. I was extravagant and enjoyed the good things in life.

Everywhere I went, people had a sense of my success and prosperity. I was perceived as a very successful entrepreneur. There was a presumption that my salary was spent on a lavish lifestyle and the latest fashion trends. However, my biggest expenditures were more toward charities, fair-trade businesses, and technologies. I also appreciated art and history, and I spent more on items that carried a historical or cultural value. I chose to spend in these areas generously.

The luxury image begets luxury. I was expanding *lebua* in ways that would make it a globally recognized brand. I was out to create history in hospitality. The idea for my business model evolved from just food and beverage service to creating an emotional experience.

From the time I took on the role in 2003/2004, my methods were unheard of and had created some ripples in the industry. The Bualerts and I continued to expand the business into what would eventually become *lebua*. For the next three years, my ultimate goal was to create and rebrand *lebua*'s image to be synonymous with luxury hospitality.

The *lebua* hotel brand was a newcomer. In a highly competitive and saturated tourist hotspot like Bangkok, I was out to make a name through unique and creative methods. I was giving luxury a new meaning; it was an experience not a price tag. And for that, I was willing to take risks that most people would shudder to even consider.

My belief is that life's truest luxuries are built around perfect moments of sensory experience, not on monetary value. This is what I was out to prove. But I had yet to find the perfect idea that I could translate into reality.

One day, in February, 2006, it came to me.

My belief is that life's truest luxuries are built around perfect moments of sensory experience, not on monetary value.

I was on one of my regular travels to and from Bangkok, on a flight with Robert, a colleague and friend. We share a common passion for hospitality and in no time, we were deep in discussion, exchanging the latest trends in our industry.

While flipping through the in-flight magazine, Robert noticed an advertisement for a 10,000-baht dinner organized by a well-known restaurant in Bangkok. We discussed the feasibility of such a dining experience. Apparently the 10,000 baht, or the equivalent of US$285, dinner had received a poor response and was considered expensive.

Expensive?! I thought it was a fabulous deal, as long as the meal lived up to the hype.

While we had our drinks, I was quite ignited by the 10,000-baht dinner and the potential to create a statement.

"Robert," I said, "What if we planned a dining experience? What would we price it at?"

He grinned. "Deepak, you have that "wild idea" expression all over your face."

I laughed. "Yes, of course, it is an idea that fits with our *lebua* brand ..."

Robert looked at me seriously. "These kinds of exclusive dinners are hard to organize. Very often they are not worth the effort."

"Come on, Robert ... think big, we can create a rippling effect and it will add value to the *lebua* luxury experience. We can make it happen! What would you say we could price it at?"

"Maybe 40,000 ... maximum 50,000 baht." He replied hesitantly.

I laughed. "My dear friend, let's think bigger! More like a million-baht dinner. We are not serving just food and beverage, but a once-in-a-lifetime experience."

He joined in the laughter thinking I was joking.

"Robert, I am serious," I said.

And that's how the idea was born.

My goal was to create a once-in-a-lifetime inspirational event, a culinary work of art—something people would remember for years to come.

While writing this book, the Million Baht Dinner is still considered to be the most unique emotional experiential dinner in the world. I wanted to create a rare experience by bringing in the best people in their field—Michelin starred chefs, master sommeliers, and other culinary experts to put together a gastronomic experience under one roof. People are willing to pay the price for this type of exclusivity to have the pleasure to taste the best of the best. This concept took time to sink in with the stakeholders, but once I got the green light, I was full force ahead.

It took nearly a year to get the Million Baht Dinner organized. It was promoted as part of the "Epicurean Masters of the World," depicting Thailand as a great destination for the super-rich. Every tiny detail was taken into account. From the guests' arrival and stay, to their privacy, service, and discretion, it was all part of the package. We were not out to flaunt this event; we were focused on creating an experience for those who paid for it. Every aspect was meticulously studied. The suppliers of the ingredients were vetted, the transportation and storage planned out, and every food item checked for quality and standards.

No expense was spared to ensure that the high achievers from the United States, Europe, the Middle East, and Asia had the experience of a lifetime, many of whom still talk about it even today, fifteen years later. The guests' identities were kept secret; no photos were taken, and all the mobile phones were kept away in order to maintain exclusivity. The *lebua* legendary dinner resulted in a buzz of publicity. The world took notice.

The Million Baht Dinner gave a perspective that in Thailand, luxury and backpackers could co-exist. It created opportunities for the backpackers to become future luxury consumers. The tourist destination remained the same, but the people's perspectives of Thai tourism and the way they experienced it changed. That was an indicator of the diversity of Thailand.

While this lavish affair brought attention to Bangkok, it also brought some negativity from the locals, who believed that the authentic experience of the city was in sitting at a folding table in an outdoor street side stall. While that may be true for some tourists, selling a meal is different from selling an experience. There are certain people who are interested in a different kind of dining style. We were offering a specific kind of emotional experience in a destination hotel.

The situation took a drastic turn when a week before the event, I received a call from the BBC asking for an interview regarding the dinner. While I was being interviewed, which went on for an hour, the reality of my current situation hit me—this big fancy dinner event could go either way. There was a lot riding on this event. Everything would be noticed and analyzed. The thought of it was overwhelming. Despite sitting in my air-conditioned office, after the interview was over, I was drenched in perspiration. Ruminating on all that I had said to the BBC, I was even more ardent in my desire to make this dinner event worth remembering.

When the BBC newswire published the article, suddenly my name and the Million Baht Dinner was all over the news. It was as if an Oscars was about to happen. I was receiving nonstop calls from the media asking for interviews, details of the menu, the guest list, and whatever else I had planned. Well-known publications wanted to write a feature and others wanted to report live to their news channels. The buzz was electric, I could feel the energy in my bones.

The morning of the Million Baht Dinner, over forty international press and media journalists were setting up video cameras in the hotel lobby. At 6:00 p.m., when the event was about to start, CNN was the first to cover it live. We had a strict privacy policy. The press was not allowed past the lobby. We maintained that the guest list was confidential, and we had ensured it to maintain their privacy. Still, the press didn't leave the venue, and continued to report from outside the hotel.

On the 10th of February, 2007, on the 65th floor of the *lebua* hotel, at Mezzaluna restaurant, diners were welcomed with a thirty-minute firework show, a shower of rose petals, a glass of the best champagne, and then the heart-stopping ten-course signature menu (listed below). This meal was created by six chefs with three Michelin stars each. It was the ultimate in sensory pleasure. Each dish was a work of art. The guests tasted the world's finest wines, were treated with gifts, and were gifted an overnight stay at the hotel.

THE MENU[3]

First Course
Meal Crème brûlée of foie gras with Tonga beans
Wine 1990 Louis Roederer Cristal
Chef Alain Soliveres from Taillevent in Paris, France

Second Course
Meal Tartare of Kobe beef with Imperial Beluga caviar and Belon oysters
Wine 1995 Krug Clos du Mesnil
Chef Antoine Westermann from Le Buerhiesel in Strasbourg, France

Third Course
Meal Mousseline of "pattes rouges" crayfish with morel mushroom infusion

3 "What Does a $25,000 Menu Look Like?," NBCNews.com (NBCUniversal News Group, February 10, 2007), https://www.nbcnews.com/id/wbna11497252.

Wine 2000 Corton-Charlemagne, Domaine Jean François
      Coche-Dury
Chef Alain Soliveres from Taillevent

Fourth Course

Meal "Tarte fine" with scallops and black truffles
Wine 1996 Le Montrachet, Domaine de la Romanee-Conti
Chef Antoine Westermann from Le Buerhiesel

Fifth Course

Meal Brittany Lobster "Osso Bucco"
Wine 1985 Romanee-Conti, Domaine de la Romanee-Conti
Chef Jean-Michel Lorain from La Cote Saint Jacques in
      Joigny, France

Sixth Course

Meal Ravioli with guinea fowl and burrata cheese with a
      veal and truffle sauce
Wine 1961 Chateau Palmer
Chef Annie Feolde from Enoteca Pinchiorri in Florence, Italy

Seventh Course

Meal Saddle of lamb "Leonel"
Wine 1959 Chateau Mouton Rothschild
Chef Marc Meneau from L'Esperance in Vezelay, France

Eighth Course

Meal Sorbet "Dom Perignon." Supreme of pigeon en croute
      with cepes mushroom sauce and cipollotti
Wine 1961 Chateau Haut-Brion
Chef Heinz Winkler from Residenz Heinz Winkler in
      Aschau, Germany

Ninth Course

Meal Veal cheeks with Perigord truffles

Wine 1955 Chateau Latour

Chef Heinz Winkler from Residenz Heinz Winkler

Tenth Course

Meal Imperial gingerbread pyramid with caramel and salted butter ice-cream

Wine 1967 Chateau d'Yquem

Chef Jean-Michel Lorain from La Cote Saint Jacques

After the event was over, I was both exhilarated and exhausted. I recall a comment by a guest that made all the months of planning, preparation, time, and effort worthwhile. He commented, "This dinner isn't just an experience of a lifetime, but a bargain of a lifetime."

In one particular AP article, it was reported that even though the dinner was expensive, it was worth it for the experience. The article pointed out that there was nowhere else in the world that you could get such amazing Michelin-starred chefs and the pairing of foods with such exemplary wines, as well as being treated with such respect and reverence, all under a single roof. My idea of luxury was expressed through this dinner, and people finally began to agree with me: Luxury is not a price tag—it is an experience.

Luxury is not a price tag—it is an experience.

Most of the profits from the Million Baht Dinner went to Medecins Sans Frontieres and toward the Chai Pattana

Foundation, a rural development program set up by the King of Thailand. These charities provided clean water and books to disadvantaged rural communities. This hadn't been the original plan, but a reporter who interviewed me was the one who inspired that decision. When he asked if it was going charity, I realized that it was a great idea! So we implemented it. The expats appreciated my work, and the media was eager to know what was next. There was respect for my vision and methods. From a well-known person in Thailand who opened a rooftop restaurant, overnight, I had become a recognized personality worldwide. I was a man with food and beverage management skills; however through my innovative ideas, I'd changed what luxury meant. In a way, I invented a new perception of service. With efficacy and economics, I added value toward the *lebua* brand, proving in certain ways that the impossible is possible. The first time I shook up the industry was when I envisioned a rooftop restaurant and then the Million Baht Dinner. I changed the whole model of running a hospitality chain.

THE SUCCESSFUL FAILURE
THAT FOLLOWED

It is human nature for us to often doubt an unusual or never-been-tried-before idea. Any new concept takes time to create trust and understanding. Whenever I wanted to improvise on a service process, in order to raise the bar toward a better customer experience, there was risk of failure. But by trying and failing, one becomes better. We are all here to offer a higher quality of service. The ultimate goal is to provide the best experience.

After the huge success of the Million Baht Dinner, I wanted

to try something new while helping the less fortunate at the same time. I had planned another specialty dinner as a charity function to bring funds and needed supplies to poor villages. However, some people viewed the event differently. The media termed it "emotional tourism." There were considerable critical comments in the press, which led to several chefs backing out of the project. I was briefly overtaken with fear. I felt that my years of hard work would be destroyed by a few negative articles. But I persisted. There was never the option to not do it, so I just had to find a way to make it work. To my relief, the negative press did not affect us adversely. Our customers trusted us; they still believed in us and remained loyal.

By trying and failing, one becomes better.

It was an eye-opening moment. I had made the decision to plan this charity dinner from a place of sincerity and generosity. I wanted to create a form of tourism that would help the less fortunate. But others did not view it through that same lens. That's why I call it a successful failure. The negative press did not derail the project, and our clients were happy and remained loyal, but it wasn't the success I had hoped for. I think our clients recognized our effort and what we were trying to do, even if it didn't have the effect we originally intended. I realized then that people are more forgiving of mistakes than we would like to think.

This dinner did not have the impact that the Million Baht Dinner did, so it was time to move on to other ideas and new projects. But I learned that as I keep putting my best step forward and power through the fear, I am always growing and developing my strengths while overcoming my weaknesses.

FINAL THOUGHTS

The Million Baht Dinner was a resounding success. It was a defining moment in my career. It was something never before attempted, but it ended up being an experience that the attendees still talk about to this day. I wanted to show the world that luxury is an experience, and this dinner accomplished that. It came to define innovation in the luxury space, which has always been a goal of mine. I was really riding high, and people were emulating my model of service and luxury around the world. I guess the one thing I want you to take away from this chapter is that with conviction (especially in the face of naysayers), hard work, innovation, and a little creativity, you can accomplish almost anything.

On the flip side of that, I also know that ego can get the better of any of us. I didn't know it then, but that moment was coming for me. I've always been an achiever, but even in this hyper-competitive market, I have never taken my achievements for granted. Don't get me wrong—I do enjoy the compliments and accolades, but for me, it is a one-day celebration, then back to work the next day. I was eager to get started on the next project, which I was *sure* would be a success. Little did I know . . .

In many ways the hospitality business is transparent. Competitors can see if you have made a mistake or if you have earned accolades. We are judged by experts on how we could do things better. And anything that is successful is quickly copied. What is an innovation one day is commonplace the next. I know better than most that once you get complacent, it doesn't take long for an eager competitor to replace you. Yet, in the next chapter I will share with you how I forgot several of the lessons I'd learned throughout my career as I sought to replicate my success in new markets.

Chapter 9

WHEN GOOD IDEAS GO WRONG

I believe that certain failures provide opportunities to gain new levels of understanding. If you lose sight of certain vital aspects of a project, it can lead to failure. From my perspective, I have an innate faith in the potential of people, and therefore trust easily. At times, having this kind of trust does not turn into a positive outcome (as I learned with the Singapore project.) In terms of how I work on any project, I always put in 101 percent. But if you lose sight of your customer, 101 percent means nothing. That is what happened to me in Frankfurt.

After the success of all the Dome restaurants and bars, the Bualerts and I wanted to look into expanding to new markets. I knew the managing director of a German hotel chain and we got in touch with him. I saw it as this great opportunity to move out of Thailand and into Europe. I thought, *At least there's somebody I know, so we'll be in safe hands.* We began looking for locations and putting together the project.

We found a historic building that had previously been a Japanese restaurant. However, because it was a heritage site, we had to get a lot of approvals for the changes we wanted to make.

This ended up being more problematic than expected. Still, we moved forward. We hired the best designers, and we hired a construction company that was at the top of their game. Everyone we hired was at the top of their game, with price tags to match. Some people in our company told us not to hire those vendors because we were spending money for a restaurant and the investment would be huge. They said it would be very difficult to make money on the project.

We didn't listen. We didn't listen to anybody. Or more to the point, *I* didn't listen. Remember how I said I lost sight of those lessons I'd learned previously. This was the first one. We ignored our colleagues and our advisors, and said we wanted to do it anyway. Admittedly, the restaurant came out beautifully—in fact, it won a prestigious design award. But what it didn't do was make money.

We opened Frankfurt Breeze to great fanfare. The Pan-Asian restaurant was going to be a huge hit. All our experience and analytics told us it would be. It attracted the right demographics for our market. We were replicating a successful concept that had already been tested in Asia. We had a prime location. Everything pointed to success. I had put in a lot of energy and hard work into making it work. In those early days, the restaurant was full, and we thought we had pulled it off. However, it did not last.

So why didn't it make money? If I am being very honest and transparent with myself, I think it was a lack of planning on my part. I didn't understand the regulations of Frankfurt or how much time it takes to get work permits, or how much time it takes to get the licenses, or how other things could cause delays in the construction. My team and I had been so successful on all our other projects that it gave us the confidence, overconfidence really, even in the face of major setbacks. We thought, *We are known everywhere, every other magazine has written about us.*

We are known as masters of the full beverage experience. How can we be wrong? We cannot be wrong.

I'm a marketing person, and I thought we could come up with the perfect marketing plan to make it all work out in the end. We painted a train with the Breeze logo. We hired the top marketing firm. We spent money left, right, and center. But as time went on, things just got worse.

It has taken me a few years to realize that it had nothing to do with anyone else. It was pure arrogance . . . overconfidence. A lot of success had gone to my head. We also had some other setbacks. A week after we opened, there were electrical failures which set off the fire alarms. The restaurant had to be emptied. We were full at the time and had to evacuate and close down for the day. That was a real blow. For many years, I blamed those issues for Breeze's failure, but it was really a combination of some unfortunate events and my ego and overconfidence that made Frankfurt Breeze an unsuccessful operation. Later, I realized that the European market was different. People said about me, "Let's see what he is going to do. Yes, he's pulled off some successful businesses but this is a different country, different people, different tastes, different culture." I ignored it.

I mention that my team and I were responsible. That's true, but at the end of the day, the failure is on me, and me alone. It is Me, Incorporated, LLC, Limited Liability Company. It was my arrogance in not respecting the local cultures, and not understanding their timelines. And the time it takes with the local laws. Beyond that, I also forgot the cardinal rule. Remember your customer. I'd been advocating all over the world that we are a customer-oriented organization, but at this junction maybe too much of success went to my head, and I forgot the customer comes first.

Germans are very particular people. Frankfurt may be a

banking city, but the people there value simplicity. Simplicity is more important than living the high life, which is the opposite of what we'd experienced in our Asian markets. We went with big marketing, flashing big money. I think we scared the customers. And Germans are rich, but they don't believe in showing off their wealth. They maintain an aura of quiet elegance. We lost sight of that and flashed our money.

We hired staff from the best restaurants. We paid them exorbitantly. They also came to believe that arrogance is the way to show their success and high pay. The staff was very entitled. They had the attitude of, "If this customer is complaining, let him complain. It doesn't matter to us." This type of attitude always trickles down. And it was trickling down to everyone in the staff. We misinterpreted the whole service experience.

We made a mistake with the menu, too. We went in thinking that Europeans wouldn't be used to the spice level we have in Asia, so we used less spice. But our customers weren't interested in that. They wanted an authentic experience—they wanted food exactly like they'd had when they traveled to Asia. We, or really, I, forgot to take the time to understand our customer.

We, or really, I, forgot to take the time to understand our customer.

Finally, when we were hit with all the electrical problems and fire alarms (and on Christmas Eve and New Year's Eve, no less!), we didn't reach out to our customers and offer our apologies and a raincheck for them to come back. Basically, everything I'd advocated for in terms of customer experience fell short on this project. It was ego and overconfidence, it was not taking the time to understand the customer, and it was a failure to remember my past lessons.

It was a very expensive lesson.

ACCOUNTABILITY

It took me a long time to come to terms with my own part in Breeze's failure. Longer than I'd care to admit, really. I failed myself when I didn't take accountability for what happened. It was easier to blame the fire alarms, etc. But that didn't serve anyone well, least of all me. I just needed to stand in front of the mirror, look at myself, and realize it was me. But when I did, I turned to introspection to try to discover the lesson from this experience. The obvious one was to remember what I'd already learned, and not let ego and arrogance overwhelm good sense. But I felt there was more to it.

The answer that eventually came to me was that there was a lack of focus.

Then I asked myself, *But what is focus?*

How does one define this simple, yet powerful word called "focus?" The dictionary offered varying definitions; some were from a scientific perspective, and others had a more behavioral description. I picked one that seemed relevant. It described focus as "a point of concentration" or "directed action." For me, that was still vague; it didn't pinpoint exactly what it meant to have focus. In reality, from my experience, focus was connected to something much deeper within me.

I needed clarity. I turned to biographies of well-known personalities like Barack Obama. He explained that focus was necessary to achieve anything worthwhile in life. The Blackstone Group's chairman, Stephen A. Schwarzman, also explained that focus is an important trait in business. But none of them gave a clear indication of what it meant to actually *have* focus; their perspectives came from different contexts. A friend who is an executive coach recommended meditation. I asked him how much time do I need to meditate? He replied that it would take two years, and still, I may not get clarity on my definition of focus. That really didn't help me.

It is said that when the mind is involved in mundane tasks, the subconscious gives us the answers we are looking for. That's what happened for me. Out of the blue, it just came to me.

One evening, while I was washing the dishes, in the quiet of my kitchen, I became lost in thought. I didn't even realize how long I had been standing there. My wife came in and saw that the water was steaming hot, and I was oblivious to it. She quickly turned off the tap. My hands were red from the scalding water. I hadn't even felt it. I was standing there washing that one dish for forty-five minutes contemplating on a single word.

I had been thinking about a scene from an ancient scripture. In the five-thousand-year-old story of the Mahabharata, Arjuna had to shoot an arrow in the eye of the fish from a great distance. He had to have laser focus. A very interesting aspect of Arjuna's story came to my attention. The moment when Arjuna was aiming his arrow at the eye of the fish, he became conscious of his weaknesses which distracted him. He'd discovered his weakness was impatience. To regain his focus, he had to accept this weakness and move forward in spite of it.

That, for me, is the meaning of focus: consciousness of one's weaknesses. Until you recognize and acknowledge your weaknesses, you cannot achieve success. The moment of consciousness of one's weaknesses is the moment of truth. That is the moment when you can convert your distraction to make it your strength. If one's focus is lost in the haze of success, or praise and recognition, the ego takes over and one's weaknesses can lead to mistakes.

Another important point came from Mr. Narendra Modi, the Prime Minister of India. Sometime after he had won the second round of elections, he spoke about (and I'm paraphrasing here) how we as humans will make mistakes; that we are fallible. The fear that comes from making mistakes will then lead to more mistakes. However, when critics see the hard work behind these mistakes and the conviction and sincerity in achieving an altruistic goal, there is forgiveness. It is a powerful truth of human nature—that forgiveness comes readily to the surface when we see people struggle and fail. We forgive them because we know they tried their best. They put every ounce of strength toward achieving a positive outcome, but still they failed. It is human instinct to value hard work, to admire sincerity, and to forgive.

It is human instinct to value hard work, to admire sincerity, and to forgive.

Over the years I've developed a philosophy on what it means to focus, but that process really started here, in this moment when I most needed it. There are many people who have shared their definition and experience about what it means to focus. When I have trouble focusing, I ask people how they like to do it. They come up with solutions like yoga or meditation. For me, I have learned that focus lies within me. It comes from our own state of mind and an awareness of our strengths and weaknesses. It is the ability to not get carried away by praise, to stay humble, and continue on the chosen path toward a goal. When you become conscious of your own weaknesses, that is when you will gather your strength, and you will find the focus you need to work toward your goals . . . just as I did.

FINAL THOUGHTS

If I were to give any advice on the subject, I would say it is that you shouldn't amplify your failure by explaining it to anyone, because the world is not going to understand. If you amplify your failure, it clearly shows you are not convinced that you have failed because you keep justifying and defending your actions. It doesn't matter that you have failed, so accept it gracefully and move on. From there, ideas will come.

Failure is an organic part of success; it is not that one must fail, but with failure one gains wisdom and overcomes fears. Sometimes a seemingly unimportant issue can change the whole landscape of a project. Such pockets of vulnerabilities exist in any business plan. We must not presume that experience and knowledge guarantee an outcome of success or victory. Sometimes, mistakes happen. The point is to take it as a lesson and move on.

We must not presume that experience and knowledge guarantee an outcome of success or victory.

The other piece of advice I would offer is something I myself took away from this experience. Keep a journal and only write very rarely in that book. That notebook should have each of the lessons you've learned throughout the years. Lessons from successes, but most of all the lessons learned from failures. Track anything new you are trying and the result or the lesson learned from it. Any time you are working on a new endeavor, open that book and read it. Don't forget your basic lessons like I did.

Today, I keep that book by my side any time I do anything new. I read it and I remember that I have to be humble. I have to be grounded. I remember that the customer comes first. I remember to listen. And to ignore fear. I need this reminder because sometimes you never know when you will forget. Sadly, there is no GPS to life. But for me, this little notebook is the next best thing.

Decision-making is not about being right or wrong, it is an art. The most important aspect of art is the perspective, because when you look at art from different angles there will be differing viewpoints. The strength lies in understanding one's vantage point. And even though Breeze failed in Germany, it didn't mean I would stop my pursuit of excellence.

Chapter 10

TRANSCENDING TRENDS

There are many unspoken, arbitrary standards in the hospitality industry. A person from a private school is usually given more respect and valued more, while others who don't fit in such categories are often underrated and underappreciated. We often avoid sharing our pasts, especially when we are socializing with a different class of society. But there is no need to be ashamed of your history. You should be proud of your roots because that's where your creativity begins. The unique and out-of-the-box ideas come from a mental space that is unrestricted by old standards.

The way I define luxury is a quality that is a class apart, a kind of simplicity and genuineness that is unique, yet charming and evocative. I have always had more reasons to challenge the trends rather than follow them. This street-smart resiliency in pursuing my own ideas is what fueled my trajectory to success. A lot of it had to do with my upbringing.

As much as I respect my father, I am very different from him. My father, when he was fifty, valued job security. He was the kind of man who did not believe in taking risks. He was thrifty and would ensure that we didn't have to borrow money for the month. He scrimped and saved every rupee. Over the years, this constant worry about monthly expenses eventually took a toll on him. I vowed that I would develop my abilities and follow a career path where I wouldn't have to worry about money. I wanted to be like my father in terms of his honesty, humility, his thought processes, and his intelligence, but I didn't want to be like him in how he worked so hard to make ends meet.

I have always had more reasons to challenge the trends rather than follow them.

I wanted the life on the other side of the street. The one I saw at Mr. Pathak's home, or one of even greater luxury. And that has given me a better understanding of the luxury experience, and that understanding has impacted how I've designed my restaurants and bars. To explain this a bit further, we will have to go back in time just a bit, to before the Frankfurt Breeze, and even before the Million Baht Dinner. We will start just after the launch of Sirocco.

In 2004, barely a year after Sirocco's launch and success, I set my sights on new horizons and was taking risks. My goal was to create a different kind of hospitality trend. My latest creations, the Distil bar and the Mezzaluna restaurant, were under construction. Unlike Sirocco and Sky Bar, which were both located outdoors on the rooftop of *lebua*, Distil was going to be an indoor bar. I had already mapped out a different perception for Distil. It was a challenging project. The bar scene in Bangkok was doing well in luxury hotels. Distil, if I were to analyze it honestly, had nothing new to offer as a bar. Sky Bar had the view, so did Sirocco. Distil was indoors, with a small terrace which we used as a cigar bar. Distil could end up being like any other bar in Bangkok. I couldn't let that happen.

So I created a plan for how it would be perceived differently, and therefore stand out from the rest. While the approved color scheme for Distil was red and gold, I changed it to black and copper. I also wanted the seating to be facing inward toward the center and focused on the experience of the bar itself, rather than the view. Distil's guests would not be facing the spectacular view. If a guest wanted to look at the view, they would have to turn their heads. Everyone thought it was a foolish idea. I thought differently, (surprise, surprise!). I thought, let's give people beauty in small doses and they will find more pleasure in it. You take for granted something you see all the time or for hours on end. You appreciate the small moments of exceptional beauty. My interior designer was not happy with my ideas but went along with what I wanted.

There were many comments by critics that Bangkok was already saturated with bars that were popular hotspots for a short period of time. There would often be long queues outside the new venues when they opened, but six months later the interest would fizzle out and often those bars would become empty. Therefore, the biggest acid test for me was to see how Distil faired in that kind of hyper-competitive environment.

First of all, I decided that Distil's highlight would be exclusive whiskeys and cocktails, which meant I needed something top of the line. I wanted brands like Royal Salute and Chivas Regal. My purchase manager connected with various suppliers and distributors. At that time, Pernod Ricard, a worldwide producer of wines and spirits, was recognized as one of the biggest liquor companies. I requested a meeting with the managing director in Thailand. It wasn't easy. He had a busy schedule and was only available for a half hour in between meetings that day. I accepted. If I only had thirty minutes, I would make the most of it.

I met him; we said our hellos and I was quick to express my desire to do business with him and his company. It turned out to be one of the easiest negotiations. That thirty-minute meeting extended until late into the night. We had dinner, entertainment, and business discussions. But it was one of my most memorable and pleasurable meetings I've ever had. And as a point of note, our long-term partnership has been profitable for both of us. Even today, our company is featured in Pernod Ricard's annual report.

We also partnered with Coca-Cola distributors. Our pricing policy was different. Our goal was to encourage guests to try out the different cocktails that were offered at Distil. If they wanted a Coke, it would be available, but it would be the most expensive soft drink in the country. We priced it at $12. For a single soda. Beers, soft drinks, and wine by-the-glass were all priced in the higher range. Unlike other hotels, where the wines that were served by the glass were cheaper in quality, we offered only the exclusive, high-end wines by the glass. Therefore, the prices were higher. The kind of people who were drawn to Distil were high-flyers, wealthy businessmen, and like-minded individuals. Their presence turned Distil's ambience into an exclusive club.

EQUALITY ... AGAIN.

In June, 2004, when Distil was launched, we received an excellent response. Around that time, a family friend of the owner requested that I offer a free bottle of champagne to four ladies at the bar. They had a wide social circle and were sure to bring in more customers.

"I don't need them in my bar," I responded, "Let them come, order, and pay like any other guest."

My boss's friend was shocked. "Why don't you want them to help you?" he asked me.

So I told him. "These guests will come because Distil is new. When the next new bar opens up, they will take their crowd there, away from Distil. I don't want that to happen. I am not giving anything complimentary. They will pay like any other guest."

The owner's friends went to complain to the owner, and she said, "I don't think he would do it, even for me." She shut down her friend's complaint just like that. She understood what I was trying to accomplish.

I realized that if I wanted to stay in the business, we would follow the same model as we had with Sirocco and Sky Bar and would create an emotional experience. And we would maintain the equality of respect and service to every guest dining or drinking at the Dome. There were no special favors for VIPs, celebrities, or anyone else.

Looking at the success of Distil, I was reassured that my decisions were correct. When other bars were opening and closing in a matter of months, Distil has stood the test of time. My plans were going in the right direction, and I turned my focus to the next venture.

SETTING MICHELIN STANDARDS

Mezzaluna, our Italian restaurant, was going through final touches before opening. Unfortunately, with the expenses that went into the designing of Distil and the other restaurants, our funds were rapidly vanishing. Mezzaluna's floor-to-ceiling height was six meters (eighteen feet), which was considered very high. To create the right ambience, I wanted to buy some tall glassware which would have cost about $40,000. And we only had that much left in our budget. Additionally, the interior designer wanted to create a feature wall which would cost us the equivalent of the glassware. We couldn't do both.

"I am going to make this restaurant so great that the guests will not even realize there is no feature wall," I told the interior designer. Again, he wasn't happy, but he agreed to my plan. First, I bought that tall glassware that correlated with the height of the restaurant. Then for the feature wall, I came up with the idea of spray-painted cardboard. It cost me $500 and still looks stunning to this day. Can you imagine? Trends for luxury spaces have always focused on the best of everything. I'd fall into that trap later at Breeze, myself. But at this time, I had to work with what I had. And with the right attitude and skill, anything can become artwork. Anything can become high end. That's what I mean when I say that I think differently and that we were transcending trends in the industry.

While working on Distil and Mezzaluna, I wanted to get back to the basics in a lot of ways. I realized that what was missing in the world was the simplicity. These simple things are one of the many lessons from my childhood on how to show a specific kind of sincere respect to people. Many times, when restaurants are created, the top management gets involved to hire the best interior designer, their budget is spent on the most expensive décor with chandeliers, velvet seats, feature walls, as well as the best crockery and glassware. When the restaurants are opened with a flourish, showing off the grand décor and interiors, the top management recedes to the background, and the interior designer has completed their project and moved on. The keys to this beautiful venue are then handed to a young, inexperienced manager. The point is that this kind of hospitality became ostentatious and focused on the superficial.

Mezzaluna was designed with simple themes—neutral colors portraying subtle elegance. I had an idea on how I wanted Mezzaluna to be perceived. The restaurant opened in September 2004. The menu pricing was higher than even Sirocco. The way we marketed our new Italian fine-dining restaurant was to focus on the food experience. Contrary to the belief that expensive restaurants should appear affluent with chandeliers and posh interior décor, we had a different focus.

We changed that trend to provide what a restaurant is supposed to provide: the best in food and service. The guests who dined with us most likely had even better interior décor, and more expensive crystals in their homes. In our restaurant, the simplicity was in the décor, the complexity was in the food.

Mezzaluna's central emphasis was on the simple things in life—food and service. With that focus, we had perfectionist-level attention to every minute detail. We would check every item of kitchen produce that was in the supplier's warehouse. Whenever imported supplies arrived and crossed customs, we would inspect the trucks in which they were transported. Our aim was to ensure that the whole of the product delivery and storage processes were of extremely high standards and were consistent to the quality that we vouched for.

I can say that even today, Mezzaluna serves lettuce at its freshest, and it is never stored for longer than eighteen hours. Attention to such detail was Mezzaluna's forte. I take a lot of pride in Mezzaluna. It is now a two-Michelin Star restaurant. Every chef who has worked at this restaurant has received Michelin stars. Every one! We'd set the bar very high. People who enjoy the finer things in life or have the ambition to try the finer things in life appreciate the lengths Mezzaluna goes to.

Mezzaluna would also host functions in a private room. If anyone wanted to dine there, they had to pay a $6000 deposit.

That private room was not grand. It wasn't big on décor in terms of chandeliers or artwork, but it was big on service and on providing memorable experiences. We knew what we were doing in terms of how to spend wisely. In order to command such a price, the time our guests spent with us had to be a memorable event, one that would last a lifetime, one that they would not experience anywhere else in the world. As time went by, our service was lauded as the best in the business.

But really, our secret to success was that we kept our ideals clean and simple. We paid more attention to the small details that matter the most to our guests. The fact that we were doing well was not because we were better than others. It was because we centered our approach around customer satisfaction. And as we had at Sirocco, we linked customer feedback with the training of our employees. What we were able to accomplish at Sirocco, Mezzaluna, and Distil, transcended all trends, all advice, and even transcended all our critics. I realized that everything I had envisioned had become a reality. We were a globally recognized model of hospitality.

FROM FOOD AND BEVERAGE TO HOTEL HOSPITALITY

The Hotel Suites in the State Tower were not doing well. They had an occupancy rate of around 50 percent. There was also a conflict in perception between the Dome restaurants and the hotel. At the State Tower, the hotel guests and the restaurant guests shared the same elevator. While our customers were spending $100-$200 on a meal, Hotel Suites guests were spending a meagre $60 per night for a room.

On 1st February, 2006, the Hotel Suites was acquired by the Bualerts, and it officially became the *lebua* hotel. We were all set to create our own brand in the hospitality space. We had a lavish launch party. *Lebua* was our new flagship, and I was the captain. Bangkok was now aware that Deepak Ohri was not just a food and beverage guy, but also a hotelier. They were waiting to see what I could do in this new space. Everyone else followed the norm of managing a hotel, and then opening restaurants. I was doing it in reverse.

Again, I made the biggest gamble of my life. I couldn't let this opportunity slide. I persuaded the owners, took over the hotel, and put my reputation on the line. The bold fact is that if the hotel failed, all the recognition I had achieved with the three dining establishments on the 65th floor would go down the drain.

I had a few novel ideas on how *lebua* was to be perceived. It was time to revamp and change the way the hotel appeared. I wanted to bring in a luxury feel to the rooms. After doing some customer research, we knew what needed to change. We discovered that, in a city hotel, besides being used as a place to sleep, customers hardly spent more than two hours in the room. We also knew that customers only used the phone in the room to call the operator, room service, or the concierge. At most hotels, when customers interact directly with hotel employees, those employees are junior level staff. We did the opposite. We employed our senior staff to be the face and voice of *lebua* when interacting with guests to better create the luxury experience for them.

Hospitality is not just about the service process; it is also about being vigilant in recognizing every possible weakness in the way we function. We are often our own biggest enemies because we constantly worry about what our colleagues think. Most of the time hotels are focused on what others are doing and trying to out-compete their competitors—or trying to prove a point that they are doing it better. In that whole process, the customers' needs become sidelined. When we focused on what was important, just like we did with the restaurants, we upped our game to ensure that our customers were not ignored. We created a new way of ensuring that we were serious about our service methodology. We focused on five key elements in terms of room comfort:

1. Comfortable Bedding

2. Adjustable Room Temperature

3. Bathroom Amenities and Water Temperature

4. Dining Options

5. Guest Privacy

My entire gamble in creating the *lebua* brand, as well as the restaurants, was based on intangibles. But we also revamped some parts of the tangibles. We added luxury accessories in the room. We partnered with Bulgari—unheard of in those days— to provide bathroom amenities. The bedsheets were upmarket Egyptian cotton. We improved housekeeping and other service processes.

We raised the rates as a result of the changes we implemented. *Lebua*'s occupancy dropped to 8 percent. I was being observed by my competitors, many of whom commented that just be- cause I had opened restaurants and bars, that didn't mean I would be able to run a hotel. They were right. After a few more weeks passed, hotel occupancy dwindled to just 6 percent. Many said it would take three years to develop the business model that I had envisioned.

I knew I didn't have that kind of time, so I looked into other aspects of the business. The sales team, who were originally from the Hotel Suites, were not proactive enough. They were supposed to go out and promote, but they would instead end up at Starbucks, chatting with colleagues. I asked all sixteen of the Hotel Suites sales staff to leave. This mass exodus took place three months after the launch of *lebua*. Many people laughed at me and considered it a foolish idea. I knew better.

We implemented the same business model as we did with Sirocco. We didn't need a sales team to do the sales, we needed people who had passion, belief in the product, and confidence in the management to create an impact. Instead of hiring a new sales team, we chose the restaurants' food and beverage managers to take on the role of making sales calls in the mornings. With a fleet of black BMW 7 Series limousines emblazoned with the gold *lebua* logo driving around town, we were creating a perception of class and exclusivity. Our trained managers would go from office to office to share the new vision of the hotel in the State Tower.

Lebua's occupancy dropped to a mere 3 percent. My boss looked at me questioningly. She had always trusted me, but I think even she was beginning to doubt my plan. I asked her for six months to show results. I promised her that I would make *lebua* a success. It was a promise founded on shaky ground, but I didn't let fear seep into me. I simply focused on the future.

WHEN THINGS SEEM BLEAK

It is easy to run away when things aren't going well. Fear can make us want to do many things, and that fight or flight response is very real. I didn't want to flee; I knew I needed to fight to make this a success. A film came to mind called *Lion of the Desert.* The storyline was quite memorable. *Lion of the Desert* is a 1981 Libyan historical epic war film about the Second Italo-Senussi War, starring Anthony Quinn as the Libyan tribal leader, Omar Mukhtar, a Bedouin leader fighting the Italian Royal Army, and Oliver Reed as the Italian General Rodolfo Graziani, who attempted to defeat Mukhtar.

To face the enemy, the Bedouins would tie their legs to the ground. That way, when the tanks approached, even in a momentary impulse of fear or cowardice they would not be able to back away. I realized I had to work like that. I had to hunker down and tie myself to the situation and find every possible solution to make *lebua* a success.

One day, a director of sales for a luxury hotel, a friend, invited me to coffee. He suggested taking the e-commerce route. "What?" I asked. I was clueless about this online booking system and online payments method. After spending an hour with me, explaining the ways it worked, he noticed that I was still unsure. He then suggested I hire an expert to handle my e-commerce business.

Hotel service and food and beverage is all about the human connection. If I was to bring technology into the process, would that affect my business negatively? Still, I knew that the world was connected via the internet and that there would be rapid change. I was open to all new ideas that would result in increased visibility for *lebua.*

I took my friend's advice and hired an e-commerce manager, who arranged a meeting with Expedia, one of the giants of online bookings. That was when I got my first lesson on how to improve the booking process. I immediately suggested we explore other online channels as well. I connected and built a relationship with various e-commerce websites.

We were improvising our services not just on a daily basis,

but on an hourly basis. We were fluid, willing to change and adjust to the pulse of the customer. With a carefully crafted infrastructure in place, it made it easier for me to forge relationships in other parts of the world.

> **We were fluid, willing to change and adjust to the pulse of the customer.**

During one of my travels, I stopped over in Hong Kong briefly on my way back to Bangkok. While in the airline lounge, I read an article in a magazine about the World Travel Tourism Council. They were having a summit meeting in Washington D.C. I read through the article and realized this was an opportunity not to be missed. Instead of flying back to Bangkok, I took another flight to the US. I informed my boss before boarding the flight. All she said was, "Do what you need to do, but you only have two months left."

I flew to Washington, DC, and met many people in the tourism industry. I formed a rapport with a variety of people. However, there was one hotelier who looked at me with derision. He snidely remarked, "The problem with you, Deepak, is that you are all over the place. This is a summit for those above your level. What are you doing here?"

I simply smiled at the man and said, "One day you will take back what you have said." He wasn't any better than me and I knew it, even if he did not. But still, his words, like those of other detractors before him, motivated me to do better. As karma would have it, the hotelier did come to me a few years later and asked if I would buy his hotel chain.

Shortly thereafter, our work with the e-commerce platforms started showing progress. Occupancy rose to 73 percent. I developed a promotion tie-up with a well-known credit card company, which led to exclusive deals and resulted in *lebua* gaining a high-class image. We limited our focus on social media platforms and instead focused on developing relationships with online travel agents. We were one of the first companies who got Expedia and Booking.com into the Bangkok market. *Lebua* was their first partner. We believe in online agents. At a time when other hotels were developing their own platforms and moving away from third-party booking sites, we doubled down on them.

I believe in people's strengths, and I would rather outsource and invest in talent. I was not tech-savvy, to the extent that I did not even know how I would get my money if customers booked online. I was honest about my lack of knowledge. And therefore, we partnered with those who are knowledgeable in e-commerce. I learned you don't have to be an expert in everything, you just have to partner with the right people who cover those areas where you are weakest. Our visibility and clientele grew using this model.

We ended the year 2006 with an average occupancy rate of 55 percent across the whole year; exactly what Hotel Suites had in 2005, but the daily rate doubled, profitability increased by 10 percent, and our monthly occupancy rates at the end of the year were hovering around 75 percent after we implemented those e-commerce platforms. Our food and beverage sites at that time were also doing phenomenally well. But we needed to transition to our next step with the hotel.

With a little bit of research, we also developed the best breakfast buffet. As I am writing this book in 2022, no one has been able to beat our breakfast buffet. The kind of variety, freshness, and service cannot be found anywhere else. We also extended breakfast time by an extra hour. We wanted *lebua* to be a leisure property, so we wanted our guests to enjoy the comforts of their room and then enjoy the breakfast. Customers were given the fundamental service of fulfilling their needs, and we provided what they wanted in a neat package.

Even with that change, we did not rest on our laurels. We weren't finished. Having started this journey in 2003, we kept expanding and developing. We were constantly reinventing ourselves to improve and explore new ideas. It was around that time that we did the Million Baht Dinner. We also created a new dimension to the *lebua* luxury experience with the Tower Club. Located on the upper floors of the State Tower, the Tower Club was a lounge offering five meals a day—breakfast, lunch, and high tea, with two snacks in between—and other perks for the *lebua* guests. No matter what time of day, you could always find something at the Tower Club.

EXPANDING INTO NEW MARKETS

The first two exceptional decisions that I made were to create another champagne bar, Pink, and another restaurant, The Chef's Table. Where we already had Sirocco, Mezzaluna, Distil, Breeze (Bangkok), and the Sky Bar, I was adding two more in the same brand. It seemed foolish to compete with one's existing restaurants and bars. There was a round of negative and discouraging comments. People were sure that Pink and the Chef's Table would fail.

Little do the naysayers know. Cars are cars, but models can be changed. I had a plan for my new model of bar and restaurant. I was creating an innovative concept.

Cars are cars, but models can be changed.

It's common to find a kitchen in a restaurant. My vision was to create a restaurant in a kitchen. That's how Chef's Table was born. It was a fresh perspective to create such a concept, especially one that required careful designing of the kitchen. I went all out on creating something that was modern and state-of-the-art.

I worked with the team at Electrolux and Halton. With Electrolux, we bought their aesthetically designed, Molteni custom-made stove, beautiful to look at, yet sturdy and functional. With Halton, whose board of members included Harvard and MIT professors, I worked with their team to install ionizer exhaust systems in the restaurant. At the Chef's Table, the food fumes would be converted to fresh air. The customers would not experience any residual odor of food on their attire. I used science to create a new experience for my clients, where they could enjoy watching culinary greats cooking right in front of them. This became a hugely successful idea.

And Chef's Table, for the first time in the world, received the Best Service Award by Michelin. This put *lebua* and me on a pedestal, and more than me, this positioned Thailand on the map of luxury dining destinations.

At Pink Bar, the difference that we created was that we served artisan brands to explore organic, exclusive, and unique quality champagnes. It was this perception that brought the curious and adventurous to Pink; they were willing to explore new brands. Again, we were able to attract new clients, rather than sacrifice clients from the Sky Bar. That is what matters. When we opened Pink, we earned our entire investment back in just six days. Six days!

We had created many firsts in our industry: the Otis company installed two elevators to the 61st and 62nd floors in record time. That type of elevator was the first in Asia and the fastest project that was completed in such a short span of time. With Electrolux, we were the first to modernize and customize the Molteni stoves. With Halton, we were the first to explore how to convert food fumes to fresh air. And as a result, with the right focus, we created a first-class restaurant, and added many firsts to it: including that Best Service Award. We were now ready to the next challenges, and I saw them in overseas opportunities.

In that space of awareness, we explored overseas opportunities to build *lebua*. This time I was careful, observant and took cautious decisions. I chose India, and specifically a city called Lucknow, the city where I was born. It is rich in history and culture. *Lebua* Lucknow is the first heritage hotel in the state of Uttar Pradesh.

Over time, we also noticed that many of our customers were from Australia and New Zealand. Or others were travelling *to* New Zealand. Two years later, we added a boutique hotel, an ultra-luxury lodge in Rotorua, New Zealand. It is called the Lake Okareka Lodge by *lebua* and is located in a place that is in harmony with nature, in spectacular unspoiled surroundings.

In hindsight, all our strategies seem planned and appear easy, but it wasn't. We faced many challenges. There were some issues with the *lebua* lobby which we corrected. We needed banquet rooms to accommodate large meetings for corporate business, not weddings. We didn't offer lunch as we already had a huge buffet breakfast service, but that had its own drawbacks in certain circumstances. Yet we made it work for us and for our customers.

In this way, we created our own unique service process. These systems were so strong that even today, while I'm writing this book, they work efficiently. My point here is that, with the exception of Breeze in Frankfurt (lesson learned!), we made a conscious effort to maintain a constant awareness of our customers and their evolving needs.

And with that, we are back to our original timeline.

THE POWER OF SERVICE

I recall a time early on in my career when I was superseded by someone else for a management position. I know how that feels. I don't like that sense of rejection, especially when their work shows results. I understand what an employee experiences when he or she is fired. My goal is to give everyone a chance to express themselves. I try to see the situation from their perspective, and then give them an opportunity to improve. My goal is to inspire, not suffocate the staff. I want them to feel comfortable enough to talk to me.

I manage 1300 employees, and deal with multiple logistical issues and personality types. But I ensure that the staff is treated with respect. They have the freedom to communicate their ideas directly with me. They have become like an extended family. Therefore, I will never fire an employee without first asking for advice from a few trusted staff members. It is not easy for me to let go of an employee; I need to make sure I am making the right decision.

I've already discussed some of my philosophies regarding hiring practices. In the service industry, when executives hire staff, they look mainly at the résumé/CV and background experience. They generally say if you don't have the right experience, they cannot hire you. I, however, don't place too much importance on CVs. Instead, I look for something unique in the individual. I want to see some of the traits I value most in myself—that eagerness to learn, that ambition to grow, that passion for their work. In any field, passion is important to build oneself up, and believing in a brand like *lebua* motivates the staff to serve. I want my staff to feel inspired every single day at work.

Until 2010, I handled all hiring myself. When I'm hiring, I want someone who perhaps never got the opportunity to work in a luxury organization. When we were hiring for the first champagne bar, I hired a woman who I found selling KFC chicken. Normally I would ask my secretary to go pick up the KFC, but one day I went there myself with my colleague and we stood in the queue. I noticed how the girl behind the counter was talking to each customer. She was very friendly and professional, and yet she was just selling chicken. I said to my colleague, "Look at the service she's giving. She should be someplace else." I was so impressed by her that I gave her my card and offered her a job on the spot. I even had my assistant follow up with her.

When I hired her, her English was not that great. But I said, "Don't worry, we'll give you English lessons. We'll pay for them." I invest in my employees, especially when I see such potential. And my investment in her certainly paid off. She ended up selling the most champagne of all our staff. Can you tell me one other hotel in the world which would hire a lady from behind the KFC counter to sell $150 glasses of champagne? But it worked.

I also have made a habit of hiring nurses. They are very caring individuals and tend to be excellent servers. How do I lure them away from their current jobs? Simple. I pay them more. And I invest in my employees. It encourages loyalty. Of the original eleven employees at Sirocco, eight are still working for me. One is a manager, one invested in the business, another we sent off to train to be a sommelier. With the right people, investing in them is a sound policy. Even if they were to leave, it's okay because the idea is to make sure that wherever they go, the customer gets great service. I just have a sense for people, and it pays off. It is a skill everyone should try to cultivate.

I can sense if an employee is down or uninspired—usually they have personal issues or struggling with some aspect of their job. Just by body language I can tell if the employee has some issues. And I make it a point to invite them in for a one-on-one chat. This empowers the bond and loyalty within the corporate culture. It is about mutual respect and understanding that everyone has some good days and some bad.

Our employees are the strength of our hospitality industry. They are our greatest asset. If they are treated with respect, they will behave the same with our clients. And that's an important part of the work culture. A sincere approach toward the customers who step into the *lebua* world is vital to creating a positive experience. That starts with employees. One of the ways we keep that standard up is our staff cafeteria. We have the same food there as we do in the restaurant. How else are employees going to be able to describe the food if they don't taste it for themselves? I remember when I was starting out, I was mocked for not knowing wines, or certain foods, or high-end brands. I would never want my staff to feel what I felt in that situation.

Another thing we do differently lies in how we trust our employees. Many other companies say that they trust their employees. But then they will do mystery audits. Audits cost 1/10th the price of customer research. And it is faster. But I always have refused to do a mystery audit because it's breaking their trust. I've had senior executives tell me, "Oh, you can break your word because the employees always break theirs." So I said to them, "Employees can afford to break their word. But as an organization, we cannot." That is a fundamental piece of our philosophy at *lebua* and what sets us apart. We have to rise above the common philosophy of distrusting our employees and do better ourselves if we want our employees to do the same.

Another piece to that puzzle is care. If you don't care about your people, how can you ensure they care about your customers? At *lebua*, as CEO I get the same amount of vacation as the dishwasher. My medical plan is the same as his, too. We also don't offer part-time positions because it would be disrespectful to have them working for us without access to the same benefits that full-time employees get. We care, and in return, our employees extend that care back to us and back to our customers. We have a mutual respect.

At *lebua*, we are careful about how we are perceived and maintain a balance of staying exclusive while still being approachable. In that regard, we keep client privacy as one of the primary competencies at *lebua*. We often receive bookings from guests who are celebrities and wish to remain out of the media. We accommodate them fully with this request. Our staff are trained to maintain discreet and noninvasive behavior with *every* guest, not just celebrities.

A journalist from a glossy magazine once visited us, and I suggested that he do a feature on *lebua*. He responded with, "First, you need celebrities to visit your hotel." While we were having this conversation in the restaurant, two celebrities were dining there. His eyes popped. He'd never realized that we already had celebrity guests staying with us. That was by design. It was because we value privacy and comfort for ourselves and our guests. I believe that if you are natural and give your guests space, it fosters a sense of comfort and trust. That philosophy has paid off for us. That journalist did write the article and gave us a great review—a full-page article on *lebua* and its quality of service. Celebrities like to feel that they can relax in a restaurant, and we offer that kind of discreet ambience where they can feel at ease.

Many famous faces are commonly seen dining and staying at *lebua*. Celebrities, sure, but politicians and heads of state are regular guests, too. Once, a popular singer asked if he could sing at Sirocco, and I told him no. That it was our policy not to let any outsider sing in our restaurant. He laughed heartily and said "I get offered millions to sing, and here I am willing to sing for free and you say no." You might be asking why we wouldn't let him. It's because we stick to our policies, our standards, and we treat all our guests equally. Nobody gets special treatment— or rather, everyone gets special treatment, the exact same level of special treatment.

My idea on luxury service was spawned from a book by Rohit Ramaswamy. It had a drab title: *Design and Management of Service Processes*. The author was an engineer at AT&T. I loved his concept. When I was at a previous organization that shall remain nameless, I created a design and service process report, and handed it to my boss, hoping we could implement it. He chucked the report in the trash. Here at *lebua*, I had the freedom and independence to implement and create an amazing service design. I had the liberty to make it happen. *Lebua* and our fine dining restaurants were being featured regularly in travel and tourism magazines because of it.

THE HANGOVER

It would be impossible to write about *lebua* without discussing the movie, *The Hangover 2*. At *lebua*, we had never before allowed a movie to be filmed at any of our restaurants or hotels. Occasionally, we would approve still photography photoshoots to be conducted on site, but even that was rare. Our rules for this were simple: shooting had to be completed before 6:00 p.m. or after 2:00 a.m., when the restaurants were closed. And we charged US$100,000 *per hour.*

One day, the producer of *The Hangover* called me. One of the executives at the studio had given him my phone number to inquire about shooting the sequel movie at *lebua.* The producer told me, "I understand if you say no, because you have always said you don't allow filming, but we'd like you to consider allowing us to film." I thought about it and simply said, "You can't afford it."

He laughed and said, "No, really. Please, tell us a price." I quoted him the price for still photography, but made it clear we had not figured out the price for a film. I thought about it a little more and told him we had three conditions, beyond the standard pricing: First, when filming takes place, the entire cast must stay at *lebua.* He said, *"Done!"* Second, you will use our logo in all marketing in the US, Australia, and India markets. *"Done"* And third, you have to add to the script that a character writes "Meet me at *lebua,*" on his stomach. *"Done"*

We had a deal. That is how *lebua* ended up being included in all the marketing. In fact, we were the first hotel company ever to do a marketing alliance with any movie studio. We had never allowed filming before, but this was another chance to expand into a new and exciting market. To this day, people come to *lebua* specifically to hang out in the "Hangover Suite." The producer gave use permanent rights to use the Hangover name for the suite and for the cocktail, the Hangover-tini. Our bar sells more Hangover-tinis in a year than the whole of Singapore sells the Singapore Sling! It turned out to be a wonderful opportunity for *lebua,* and one that continues to pay off. I wasn't afraid to amend our policies for the right opportunity, and when you are looking to expand, sometimes the unconventional opportunities are the best.

HANDLING SUCCESS

My wife, Anita, often asks me, "My dear, why can't you enjoy your wins and celebrate your achievements? Why are you so restless to explore the next idea or business strategy? Why don't you just chill and enjoy your successes!"

I have asked myself the same questions, and I have come to realize that I have a hunger to move toward the next challenge. It is the trait of an entrepreneur who is always striving further and higher. My benchmarks keep moving upward, always looking for the next best opportunity.

When I am in a reflective mood, I do take a step back and acknowledge my strengths and weaknesses. My work is my life, and I find joy and satisfaction in every single day of being part of the service industry.

We have a great advantage that *lebua* is a smaller ship, and as the captain, I can choose to change direction swiftly. Being alert to new ways of developing have helped me grow as an entrepreneur. I believe that in business, if you want to be successful, you can't fool yourself. You get real about what you know, and what you don't know. You can't let success go to your head—easier said than done, I know. But you have to be honest about your ignorance and hire the best people who are skilled in their areas of expertise. I, too, have learned to keep the focus on the goal. I learned the hard way. Hopefully you don't have to do the same.

When we are able to admit we are ignorant, that's when the learning begins. One lesson I have learned is that there is never a right decision or wrong decision—it is all just a decision and if it doesn't work the way you want, you make the next decision, and then the next, until you reach your goal. We all work hard to make the best decisions possible, but no one has every decision work out perfectly.

*When we are able to admit we are ignorant,
that's when the learning begins.*

Having focus and a consciousness of my weaknesses has enabled me to achieve big tasks. I was creating more and building on the commitment toward *lebua's* unique customer experience. By developing and expanding my horizons, I began to realize that from my vantage point, I could see the bigger picture, and grow strategically. From "I" and "me" to a "we" scenario. It was an exhilarating feeling to see my work get so much more attention. And I admit, I enjoyed the attention.

As time goes on, we must constantly remind ourselves of the basic principles of success and failure. Each one's journey is unique and frames a different picture of how success is achieved. As an innovative entrepreneur, these experiences are not just meant to be read in books or taught in business schools. They are equally relevant as we develop ourselves. They are not only the key to finding success, but also the key to how you handle it once you get there.

EMOTIONAL CONNECTION

When social media came into existence as not just a network but as a marketing tool, everyone rushed in that direction. I didn't jump in. I was deliberately slow. I wanted to understand the concept of social networking sites and then find the best way to move forward strategically. I think social media is the biggest disruptor of people's life and privacy, so we were very conscientious about how social media would be used in our company. We are aware of its ability to create perceptions that may not work in our favor. We noticed a huge gap in our competitors' strategies in the way they each used social media. They maintained the same pricing strategy, which added to the confusion and created an entry barrier for customers rather than an obstacle for competitors.

We chose a different route.

We created a range of products with different pricing tiers in a single complex, thus creating an obstacle for our competitors to overcome. In this way, we were able to target and attract customers from different walks of life. We used strategic marketing to focus on elements unique to *lebua*, such as that we were the only hotel which had such a wide range of bars, restaurants, and atmospheres. We also trained our staff to match each unique venue. In fact, we were the only hotel in the world with two champagne bars, both successful. We did not cannibalize our business with multiple bars competing for the same customers, but rather encouraged each business to flourish by focusing on different types of customers. Not only did we attract a variety of customers, but we also increased awareness and use of our hotel. This gave us the visibility as a single destination for a full range of clients. Something we have mastered better than any of our competitors.

FINAL THOUGHTS

I've said many times that I think differently from others. This is often confused to mean thinking creatively or thinking innovatively, but that's not it at all. Not everyone can be a creative or an innovator, but we can *all* think differently. What thinking differently really means is having clarity about ourselves and about others.

I have travelled the world extensively and many people have commented that I am great at marketing, but my goal is never to market or promote. I am naturally a people person. I enjoy meeting and connecting with different kinds of individuals. I am curious about the way people behave, and my goal has always been to understand and form an emotional connection with others. Where there were salespeople and promoters who were centered around sales and marketing, my goal has always been to meet my customers and establish a relationship.

At *lebua*, there are two departments that we never had—the training and marketing departments, both of which are standard departments at every other hotel. Yet we got the Best Service Award, and Michelin stars for our high standards. We believe that we cater to a diverse range of backgrounds and nationalities, and we want to market to them. It makes no sense to have a marketing department of a handful of people who try to decide what the customer wants. Using science and emotions, we have outsourced those departments to our customers. They guide us in a sustainable way with constructive feedback that gives us all we need for both training and marketing.

Selling and promoting is not the way to build loyal clientele. From my perspective, the customer is far mightier, far more intelligent, and far more knowledgeable than we think. What customers need, in any business, is a personal connection. As long as we don't intrude on their privacy, and maintain a decorum of respect, they will trust us.

Lebua would not be where it is today if it weren't for this personal connection. It wasn't my innovativeness or my way of doing business, but more because I consciously focused on what it is that would enhance our service capabilities. It wasn't just ingenuity that enabled me to do this, I just decided to think differently. I gained knowledge from each customer I met. Many in our industry forget the difference between knowledge provider and service provider. The customer is the most knowledgeable being on the planet. We are a service provider. The day we learn the difference, that's the day we will think and act differently.

You could say that *lebua* became the umbrella under which we were catering to a global audience. We had created a synergy in our brands despite their differences. I had realized early on that having an emotional connection with a customer meant understanding their choices and desires. This whole focus on the emotional connection methodology, which we've tested many times and perfected, motivated me to speak at different educational institutions. I have visited several top universities to lecture on the subject: top institutes like Harvard Business School, Columbia, NYU, INSEAD, Kellogg and more, but this concept really served as the inspiration for creating a new course on luxury itself at Florida International University (FIU). Sharing this knowledge is important to enabling the next generation of hospitality professionals, and business professionals in general, to build a better capacity to adapt to new environments. And I am genuinely excited to be taking this next step.

I had realized early on that having an emotional connection with a customer meant understanding their choices and desires.

LIFE IS AN EXPERIENCE

In 2020, COVID-19 hit the world, wreaking havoc across the globe, creating economic devastation, and causing the loss of human lives. It wreaked havoc on the hospitality industry like nothing has before. Yet, at *lebua,* we didn't lay off a single employee.

Many people have asked, "How did you maneuver the pandemic without letting anyone go?" It's not that it was easy for us. It's going to be almost a year that we've been operating at a loss. Not many people will say that proudly, but I'm putting this on record because we should not be shy about the difficulties that we are facing. Once we express our difficulties, our challenge is out in the open, and only then can we go out and find the solutions.

So how did we handle it? We created a council, and we told the staff, we want to keep everyone, so come up with a solution. They came up with a list of deductions, which we carried out, and in the end, everyone contributed to our survival."[4]

---

4 Aiden Jewelle Gonzales, "Meet Deepak Ohri, the Visionary CEO of Lebua Hotels & Resorts," Masala Magazine, April 23, 2021, https://www.masalathai. com/meet-deepak-ohri-the-visionary-ceo-of-lebua-hotels-resorts/.

My journey has been filled with many insightful moments that were the goal posts of my life. My father's teachings formed the foundation in the way I navigated through those defining moments. He said that education and experiences are important in life, but above that, being a good human being is vital. And I would ask him: "What does it mean to be a good human being?" He replied it is caring for others, which meant being empathetic toward others' situations.

I was reminded of his teachings during COVID and how important they are. When COVID hit, we believed that the service staff were the assets of our business and letting them go would be disloyal to them. But due to the pandemic, our industry was going through turmoil trying to maintain a cost-effective approach to staying afloat. As a result, every other business was laying off their staff and downsizing. We took pride in our ability to sustain our staff. However, what we didn't take into consideration was that the pandemic had far-reaching effects, and there were major changes taking place within the hospitality industry.

While writing this book, what I foresaw was that COVID may be part of the damage, but the Artificial Intelligence industry has become and will be the ultimate cause of transformation in many businesses. From my organization, we lost 600 out of 1100 employees. They were loyal and we were loyal to them. I expected they would return after the pandemic. But by then, times had already changed. Despite the loyalty that existed between us, they left not to join a competitor, or a hospitality chain, but to an entirely different industry.

This mass exodus was a result of a change in the mindset of the future of hospitality. There was an attitude that there was no scope for growth security. It was an arresting moment of realization that none of us from the industry offered an apology to the employees who had served us for years when times were good. These men and women were the face of our industry. They worked hard, and they had been loyal to our principles and values. And yet, as they left, no one gave them a second glance.

I was under the impression that many countries would be able to support those who were unemployed. However, some countries struggled with the weight of a bad economic situation. In Southeast Asia alone, travel restrictions hit domestic tourism badly. Many families relied on a single bread winner. We were in a helpless situation where there was no support for those in our industry who became jobless. If we had foreseen the extent of the damage throughout our hospitality industry, I believe we would have been more proactive in providing a support system.

Not a single apology has been extended by any of the tourism bodies like the UN, or the WTO, or other hotel chains. That's where I believe education can bring about a social change in the culture of an organization. The idea is to lay the foundation and build a more heart-centered approach in any business. Just as my wise father had said, it is more important to use your heart to value people, to respect their efforts, and acknowledge them. Therefore, first it is important to be a good human being.

In that despair of the COVID-19 pandemic, a glimmer of hope came from the scientific community. The rapid spread of the virus was matched by the pace of scientific research to investigate measures to control the coronavirus. In a matter of months, scientific efforts gave the world vaccines and quarantine measures for a disease which was unheard of a year ago. Never before have researchers, medical experts, scientists, and others come together globally to battle a deadly virus. It was a collaboration that will make the annals of history. It is evident that for every problem in the world, the solution comes from the powerful tool that is *education*. Knowledge is proof that gives scientists the ability to save lives. Never before has science been able to act so fast and with such impact. We can see that with technological tools, information-sharing was made easier. Therefore, the latest scientific data was able to reach the far corners of the world in a matter of seconds. Bottomline: Education and collaboration is the force that can protect the evolution of humankind. I've taken this wisdom to heart, and though my industry may not have the same impact on the world that the scientific community does, education in the hospitality section still has the power to transform lives.

BIRD'S EYE VIEW

Taking a bird's-eye-view of my life, I reflect on the big picture. Looking like an observer from different vantage points gives me the clarity to understand the reality of my past. I have emphasized the value of one's roots a lot throughout this book because I believe it enables one to stay grounded. It also gives us the capacity to face certain hard truths about life, like how one is perceived by others, especially those who are not from the same background. Some may look down on us. We cannot deny the reality that not all are treated with equal respect.

The point is that if we value ourselves, we can build the kind of respect we want to see in the world. I hope that someday there will be more awareness, more acceptance, and acknowledgement that what is valued is talent and skill, not background and color.

There are many who prefer to hide their past or hesitate to share their humble beginnings. It is this desire to erase the past that troubles me. We are not changing the future by denying our past. Our origin is what defines us and gives us the resiliency to stay focused on the future. What we are today is due to that seed that was planted in childhood.

The point is that if we value ourselves, we can build the kind of respect we want to see in the world. I hope that someday there will be more awareness, more acceptance, and acknowledgement that what is valued is talent and skill, not background and color.

My ambition to succeed was evident when, as a child, I dared to cross the road to visit Mr. Pathak in the upper-class residential zone. I dared to dream big, despite the constant reminder that I am from a humble background, and I should keep my head out of the clouds. I heard many taunts from friends and relatives. It has been quite a journey of proving myself, of gaining that self-respect. In many ways, I challenged the status quo and refused to be part of society that was elitist. I am known as an idealist with a knack for speaking my truth, which at times, gains me more haters than friends. From the perspective of my friends, family, and competitors, I have achieved much. I can see it in the love and regard of my family, and I can also see it in the envious glances of competitors.

Keeping your eye on your goal, and your purpose, is what matters the most. There will be many detractors, telling you what you are doing is wrong. Listen to them, but don't deny your desire to innovate and transform to create new perspectives. The lessons I have learned during my journey to achieve my goals were tough, but they have shaped me to be stronger and more resilient and enabled me to find my truth.

In that context, I believe that we are all searching for our own truth. We look for it in the past and in the future. We look for our truth in others, we search for it while interacting with the informed and educated, and with the successful and the powerful. We can only find it when we learn from our own experiences. When we test our own limits, we can know our potential. Failing is part of the learning process. We have to go through it and discover new ways of dealing with the world that can be brutal at times.

When we test our own limits,
we can know our potential.

History can offer us a limited perspective. It has given us stories of the past, but not all of the past is based on the truth. The people who wrote ancient history were biased, and some of the "truth" that we have been told is therefore distorted. In that sense, where can we find the truth of our lives?

Is truth to be found in science? Not exactly. What science shares with us is cold hard facts. Science is about evidence-based outcomes that give us tools to apply in our lives.

If truth cannot be found in history or science, where does truth exist?

From my perspective, truth exists somewhere in between. Truth comes with realization. Within each individual's capacity to navigate through life, truth can be found. It is a self-discovery process that leads to an ability to be who you want to be.

This is how I define the truth of my life.

With that mindset, I revisit the last thirteen years. In all that time, hidden deep within my subconscious, was one powerful dream—to teach and guide others to find their truth. And here

I am, living the dream. In that moment, I knew that being true to my roots gave me the strongest foundation to succeed.

LUXURY INCUBATOR PROJECT

The Luxury Incubator Project is an MBA course at Florida International University that I helped create along with my partner, Dr. Anna Pietraszek. This experiential learning course is designed to teach students about working every aspect of a luxury brand. We've even incorporated a residency component where eighteen of these students will get to travel to New York and Los Angeles to see firsthand what makes luxury brands successful.

This is a pilot program and at the same time a flagship course for the college. To assess its success, the final outcome of the project is a comprehensive report that contains two parts: quantitative analysis conducted by a third party and qualitative analysis conducted by the students themselves. This combination constitutes the Ohri Luxury Index, (OLI) which enables us to get both quantitative and qualitative clarity on what customers want. Luxury is an evolving landscape and requires a neutral perspective.

The opportunity to teach at FIU and be a part of this project is a big honor. After many conversations and a lot of work on our next steps, I was invited to teach a class while being observed by four professors. It was intimidating, but I was not discouraged. I know my truth; I could therefore stand fully in my own to be recognized as a person of value, rich with knowledge with the ability to impact those students. I was accepted for who I am. That was one of the greatest satisfactions of my life.

Dr. Pietraszek, FIU's Faculty Fellow in Entrepreneurship and

Innovation, along with Dr. William Hardin, Dean of the FIU Business, and the other FIU faculty members all warmly welcomed me. It was a privilege for me to be part of such an elite team of educators. As I stood there, venerated, feelings of gratitude washed over me. It was time to give back what I had gained in knowledge and experience.

Throughout my career, I never hid my past, nor did I compromise on my values. This mindset enabled me to expand my thought processes. In my journey as an entrepreneur, I recalled that to understand a customer's viewpoint, it is necessary to become the customer, to put myself in their shoes of being served, instead of serving. This gave me greater clarity of the customer's needs and wants. So for this endeavor, I likewise put myself in the shoes of a student. What would an FIU student, with hopes and big dreams, who travelled from a faraway country, want to learn from me? What could I offer that is unique? That's when I hit upon an idea of what to teach for the entrepreneurship class.

On October 28, 2021, my lecture, "Entrepreneurship Through the Eyes of Luxury," became my first official visit to the FIU Business campus as the newly appointed executive-in-residence at the college's Pino Global Entrepreneurship Center.

For each letter of the word—entrepreneurship—I created sixteen guiding principles. I outlined entrepreneurship in terms of:

Efficiency

Nature

Time

Rules

Execution

Packaging

Research

Ethics

Naivety

Emotions

Understanding

Responsiveness

Self-respect

Hard work

Innovation

Perspective

These principles helped me as a businessman. I hoped it would help my students, too.

The class responded with enthusiasm. Each student thought about each principle and how it was relevant to them. Their feedback brought me a sense of satisfaction, and I looked forward to my next lecture. The dean admired my ability to explain the reality of the world in a simple manner. There was a lot of support from the FIU, which I greatly appreciated. I was enjoying teaching and I wanted to continue to inspire my students.

At the next lecture, to a class of marketing students, I summed up one important idea: "Your weakness is your strength, and your strength is your philosophy." I also chose a case study which set the class abuzz with excitement. The three hours zipped by. The students were continuously engaged and involved in the real-life case study of Coca Cola and Pepsi Cola. I asked them if there was space in the market for a third cola. I challenged them to explore all possibilities. The students took up the challenge and even after the class was over, they continued to discuss the issue.

Your weakness is your strength,
*   and your strength is your philosophy.*

To a class of MBA students, I had the opportunity to teach a different perspective on pricing and how it was defined in different parts of the world. How would pricing affect the customer experience and how would one price the product? For this project, I divided the class into three groups, gave them each a bottle of water to price, and an hour to discuss. After that, a representative of each group was invited to present and explain their reasoning for their pricing strategy. They gave multiple perspectives, with an awareness of their thinking process, and how they arrived at their conclusion.

My own perspective and ideas were not the central theme. I could have easily shared details about *lebua* and the pricing strategies that we put in place for the different bars and restaurants. But that was just about me and my way of thinking. If I had shared my experiences, it would just be a story, and the students would lose interest. They needed to think through the problem themselves. This was an opportunity for *them* to explore and to be innovative. I taught them to probe and strategize in their own individual ways. I wanted to share my education in a way that they could understood their own values and principles first.

For example, many students aspire to go to top ranking universities. If they don't get accepted by the ranked universities, they are often discouraged. I disagree with that principle. We must not measure education simply as a transactional act. Education will never fail you, but a transaction will fail. The value of education, no matter which institution, is an investment in itself. You should choose the curriculum of study over the university ranking; choose the modality or subject over a prestigious college. Many will disagree with my point of view, and that is fine. My point is for you to decide what you value when you are at those crossroads in your life and to look back with a sense of pride that you did it your way.

The value of education, no matter which institution, is an investment in itself.

From my perspective, education is to be revered; it is not just a piece of paper to be used as proof that you graduated, or to guarantee a job. What about your mind? Have you imbibed that which you learned? If you're only doing it for the piece of paper, maybe rethink it. That doesn't guarantee success, nor does it mean you won't find success without it—just look at me, I didn't need a formal education to succeed. Think about it; education in any form is to be used as a self-improvement tool. From there you can build yourself up, brick by brick, and become a tower of inspiration to others.

WHAT'S NEXT FOR ME

I am a firm believer that understanding our own truth can lead to clarity and better decisions. With every new endeavor, we develop an ability to achieve and succeed. With each achievement one can discover their uniqueness and their truth for their purpose in life. I genuinely respect and value the opinions of people I meet. It gives me a chance to reflect on my views. I am open to learning from others, and yet I will not compromise on what I believe is right.

I realized that the reason I was able to incite enthusiasm and excitement in my class was because I was able to show the importance of different perspectives. There are people we come across in life who are so set in their ways that they have no ability to look at the world from different vantage points. Education is the key to creating multiple viewpoints, and that, in turn, can create a more evolved democratic society. Having an open mind, and a willingness to see different viewpoints adds value in the way I share my knowledge.

As a part of the Luxury Incubator program, I invited eighteen students to visit Dior. It has become a jewel in the luxury environment, standing out on its own strength. The students shared their perspectives. These students were also invited to see the difference in a range of luxury hotels, retail shops, restaurants, coffee shops, and a mall known to be a luxury shopping destination. That is where luxury becomes a perfect combination of the qualitative and quantitative indicator of experience. It is the emotional response to the intangible. It is a rarity, and exclusivity is defined by making moments such as these stand out. The students saw firsthand the power and impact these brands and experiences provide. Education is a powerful thing.

Education is not about how much you know or how great you are because of it. The impact is created by how you can align education with the truth of your own life. The truth is different for everyone, but when people are open to learning your truth, it gives them a direction to discover their own.

Beginning in mid-2021, Dr. Pietraszek and I dedicated many hours to creating the unique luxury incubator program, specially designed to develop the luxury acumen of future businessmen and businesswomen. An official announcement was made that the luxury incubator program was being offered to MBA students to learn about luxury and my FIU affiliation was now a permanent role. I was honored when it was finally approved. It will kick-off in 2022.

When the FIU announced the Luxury Incubator MBA Project course, the news was also officially announced by the AACSB International—the world's largest business education alliance that connects educators, students, and businesses to create the next generation of leaders.

My journey, which began with the search for self-respect, has led me to discover my truth. I've never worked for commitment. I've worked by impact. Saying to my wife, "I love you, Anita," is commitment. It doesn't really mean anything without impact. But showing my love to her in small daily acts, that is *impact.* I want to take action to make an impact. That is my truth. I've done that in the world of luxury and hospitality. Now, my future goals have shifted, and I am focused on making an impact by educating the next generation of leaders in luxury.

Every night now, I look up at the sky and I see the beautiful stars—the same Bangkok sky that I had seen when I first saw the potential in Sirocco and *lebua*. But now I see in it the potential of the future generation. I know my purpose. There is so much we learn along the path, toward the bridge that leads us to our destiny. Through experiences, interactions, and at times failures, we gain wisdom. At the end of the day, A Bridge Not Too Far is a learning center, not just for those in the hospitality field, but also for those in any business. I can see the path to cross the next bridge in my journey into the future. I have arrived at the bridge that is not too far.

Appendix

REFRAMING SUCCESS

As I mentioned in chapter 9, I like to write down the lessons I've learned in a little notebook. I find this helps me revisit them and keeps me humble as I start new projects. To that end, below I've included a list of some of the lessons I've learned throughout my career. I hope you take away something from my experiences and learned something you can use on your own path to success. I've included a brief summary of many of these lessons as they have applied to me. But these are my own takeaways from *my* life. What I encourage you to do is consider each one and look for examples in your own life. Dive deep. Face your experiences honestly and see what experiences you've had that correlate with these lessons. Do you have anything you can add? Is there anything you've learned from those experiences? Take some time for self-reflection. This isn't something you need to share with anyone else. This is for *you.* And maybe someday it will be your turn to share your takeaways with the world.

1. **Remember your roots:** they are part of who you are and what makes your perspective unique in this world.

2. **Believe in your dreams:** never forget your goals and believe in your ability to achieve them.

3. Seize opportunities: opportunities arise when you are looking for them and open to them. Don't let them pass you by.

4. Embrace loyalty: inspire loyalty with everyone. Your boss, your colleagues, your employees, and your customers. This starts with respect.

5. Be diplomatic: learn to say no respectfully while still standing up for yourself.

6. Always be learning: whether or not it is in a formal setting, develop an attitude of learning.

7. Have confidence and conviction: especially in the face of naysayers. Use their negativity as the spark to motivate you to prove them wrong.

8. Trust your instincts: your gut is usually right. Believe in yourself.

9. Develop your creativity: strive to be innovative and think differently.

10. Value mentors: value the mentors in your life and remember their wisdom. When the time comes, embrace the opportunity to become a mentor yourself.

11. Small efforts yield big results: small actions are important steps on the journey to perfection.

12. Don't trust blindly: protect yourself legally and make sure you are putting your trust in the right people.

13. Be bold: don't be afraid to take risks and try new things. Don't be afraid to move on if something isn't right for you.

14. **Encourage the right culture:** participate in making a culturally neutral space where everyone feels valued.

15. **Never let fear stop you:** especially not the fear of other people's opinions. Overcome your fears and be bold in the face of them.

16. **Make connections:** build rapport with everyone you meet. And maintain those connections. You never know when it might come in handy.

17. **Listen:** listen with sincerity to those around you, experts and non-experts alike. And listen to the customer most of all.

18. **Find correlations:** look for the connections between opportunities and needs. This can be the key to finding solutions.

19. **Think differently:** open yourself up to new perspectives and look at problems from all angles.

20. **Value new perspectives:** even when you disagree. Learn to discuss issues respectfully.

21. **Focus:** be conscious of your weaknesses and move forward in spite of them.

22. **Never give up:** when things are bleak, keep working toward your goals.

23. **Failure is the best teacher:** in failure there are many tough lessons, but they are worth the heartache. Take responsibility, learn the lesson, and move on.

24. **Don't let ego overwhelm good sense:** there *is* such a thing as too much confidence. Review your lessons when starting new projects.

25. **Never forget who your customer is:** listen to your customer, understand them, and step into their shoes. This is the foundation of good service.

26. **Seek out good partners:** you can't be an expert in everything. Partner with people who cover your weaknesses.

27. **Surround yourself with the right people:** be intentional in the type of people you hire and work with. Support and invest in them.

28. **Transcend trends:** just because something is done one way by everybody else doesn't mean you can't find a better way.

29. **Experiences are better than books:** you can learn a lot from books (that's why you're reading this one!) But experiences are often more valuable. They shape your behavior and sharpen your skills in ways books can't.

30. **Strive to be the best.**

These are just a few of the principles that will help and guide you on your journey to achieve your goals, and to become better entrepreneurs and leaders of the future. These can be the starting point for your own little book of lessons. There are many more out there, so don't stop here!

ABOUT THE AUTHOR

DEEPAK OHRI, founder and CEO of *lebua* Hotels and Resorts, is well-known worldwide as an award-winning entrepreneur who has transformed the luxury hospitality landscape in Asia. Deepak Ohri is a visionary who elevated experiential luxury hospitality worldwide. He was the first to create the world's highest rooftop restaurant that has earned two 2 Michelin stars and the first to develop the concept of a vertical destination. Central to Deepak's success is his unique vision of hospitality. He believes that the focus of hospitality should be on creating lasting emotional connections for guests – his initial vision for *lebua*— which has become an industry-wide trend. He has launched dozens of successful restaurants and bars and is credited with elevating luxury hospitality in the Asian Pacific region. He created groundbreaking and revolutionary luxury-based food and beverage concepts with his extensive experience in hospitality and service process innovation. Under Deepak's leadership, *lebua* has been named the World's Leading All-Suite Hotel by World Travel Award and is rated within the top 1 percent of companies globally for customer satisfaction. International Hospitality Institute selected Deepak Ohri as one of the Global Top Most Inspirational Executives in Travel and Hospitality.

Deepak Ohri has lectured at leading business and management schools as a recognized expert in leadership and luxury hospitality, including the prestigious Indian Institute of Management Bangalore (IIMB) & ISB Hyderabad, INSEAD, Columbia University, NYU Stern Business School, MIT, and Harvard Business School. In October 2021, Deepak was appointed Executive in Residence in Entrepreneurship and Innovation at the Pino Global Entrepreneurship Center at the College of Business at Florida International University. He also serves as a Chairman of the Executive Board. In March 2022, Deepak co-designed and co-created the Luxury Incubator MBA course. This world-class course in luxury management and marketing is the first of its kind to be offered at the Graduate School of Business at Florida International University. In April 2022, Deepak joined the Advisory Board for the Center for International Business Education and Research (FIU CIBER), one of 15 CIBER centers throughout the US administered by the US Department of Education to promote US Competitiveness in International Business.

In May 2022, Deepak Ohri became an Advisory Board Member for the World Happiness Foundation (WHF), where, with a selected panel of experts, he provides strategic vision and guidance. As a result of his involvement in the WHF, Deepak created a Happiness Office at *lebua* Hotels and Resorts, assuming additional responsibilities as a Chief Happiness Officer (CHO); he emphasizes employee happiness leads to customer happiness, a breakthrough concept in the hospitality management.

Deepak Ohri is an author of a book: "*A Bridge Not Too Far: Where Creativity Meets Innovation,*" in which he demonstrates through his journey the importance of focus, self-respect, and strategic thought process. Deepak determines that no matter where one started from, success and achievement are attainable. Deepak's story highlights the pressures of a competitive service industry and how one needs to think ahead to survive and thrive. Through his experiences, he shares his inspiration to reach for the stars and cross the bridge not too far. The book is adopted as instruction material for the college-level courses in management and marketing.

Deepak's leadership and management skills are recognized and emphasized in the case study designed for management and marketing graduate students: "Lebua: Post-Pandemic Dilemmas of a Thai Luxury Hotel". The case study is ready to be released by Ivey Publishing.

Deepak Ohri has been recognized globally as an award-winning entrepreneur and celebrated speaker. He was invited to participate in the prestigious Forbes Global CEO conference both in 2008 and 2009. Deepak was a guest speaker at many prestigious events, including the Cityscape Asia Conference in Singapore, the Worldwide TRI*M Conference organized by TNS in New York, The Financial Times Business of Luxury Summit in Los Angeles, Emerging Markets Conference (REFEM) in New York, the WTTC 9th Global Travel and Tourism Summit in Brazil, Financial Times Business of Luxury Summit in Switzerland, World Travel and Tourism Council in Japan and Macau and the Tourism Forum in China, among others.

AWARDS AND RECOGNITIONS

- International Hospitality Council in association with the International Institute of Hotel Management—Lifetime Achievement Award

- International Hospitality Institute—Global Top Most Inspirational Executives in Travel and Hospitality 2021
- World Travel Awards—World's Leading Travel Personality 2019
- Asia's Greatest Brands & Leaders 2018—Global Asian of the Year 2018
- Brand Vision Award 2018—The Extraordinaire Award
- The Stars of the Industry Group 2013—THOUGHT LEADERS AWARD for Innovation in Hospitality
- The Indira Group of Institutes, India 2012—The Achievers and Leaders Award, CMO Asia & Asian Confederation of Business
- The Hospitality Asia Platinum Awards for 2011–2013: The Best in Asia Entrepreneur of The Year Award
- The Hospitality Asia Platinum Awards for 2008–2010: Most Enterprising Entrepreneur Award
- Art of Travel the Ultimate Luxury Travel Book, Netherlands 2007/2008—Entrepreneur of The Year Quality Award

NOTABLE SPEAKING ENGAGEMENTS

- INSEAD Business School, Paris
- Harvard Kennedy School, US
- Harvard Business School, US
- New York Times International Luxury Conference
- World Travel and Tourism Council, Brazil
- World Travel and Tourism Council, Thailand

- World Travel and Tourism Council, Spain
- World Travel and Tourism Council, Japan
- Entrepreneurial Summit of IIM Bangalore, India
- India Conference, Harvard
- India Conference, Columbia Business School
- INSEAD Global Luxury Forum, Switzerland
- Global Tourism Economy Forum, China
- The Economy Hotels World Asia Conference, Singapore
- Real Estate Funds and Emerging Markets Conference, NYC
- The Financial Times Business of Luxury Summit, LA
- Worldwide TRI*M Conference, New York
- Forbes Global CEO Conference, Singapore
- Cityscape Conference, Singapore
- The Hong Kong Polytechnic University
- Florida International University

TV INTERVIEWS

- Bloomberg High Flyers with Deepak Ohri
- Koktail Conversations with Nigel Oakins Episode 2 Deepak Ohri, CEO of *lebua* Hotels
- BBC The CEO EDIT with Deepak Ohri
- CNBC—Deepak Ohri on TOURISM IN THAILAND